RISKING EVERYTHING

Growing Communities of Love

Robin Greenwood

To the people of St Mary the Virgin,
Monkseaton, past, present and future

First published in Great Britain in 2006

Society for Promoting Christian Knowledge
36 Causton Street
London SW1P 4ST

British Library Cataloguing-in-Publication Data
A catalogue record for this book is available from the British Library

ISBN-13: 978–0–281–05769–6
ISBN-10: 0–281–05769–9

1 3 5 7 9 10 8 6 4 2

Typeset by Graphicraft Limited, Hong Kong
Printed in Great Britain by Bookmarque Ltd, Croydon, Surrey

Contents

Foreword

—◆•◆•◆—

'Christians are formed through a lifetime's love affair with God,' asserts Robin Greenwood, who offers this book as an encouragement to parish study and prayer groups to keep this love affair alive. His aim is to stimulate such groups to think and pray and interact together, and to discern more of their calling to serve God and the people God has entrusted us to serve.

Greenwood's concern is that churches are in danger of dying for the lack of making true and honest connections with God, one another and society. Engagement with God, each other and the world is the central theme, and the author is passionate in his belief that Christian living has to be distinctive and outward facing while open to and respectful of all humankind.

For Greenwood, discipleship begins for each of us by learning from Christ that we are infinitely and unendingly loved, blessed and forgiven and that the self-giving love at the heart of God is the pattern for all Christian living.

This is not an 'off the peg' course for parish groups. It will require prayerful and imaginative preparation by group leaders if it is to be of real benefit. It offers insights, ideas, many suggestions and helpful liturgies. Here is a rich resource for the Christian journey from Lent, through Holy Week, Good Friday and Easter, to Pentecost. This is a book that will help not only individual Christians but also parishes to keep their love affair with God well and truly alive.

+*Martin Newcastle*

Introduction

My passionate concern, through three and a half decades of ordained ministry in many settings, is for a church truly responsive to God's mission in the world. This emerging church requires an abundance, character and identity that springs from close encounters with God. Church does not exist as a fixed thing that travels through the centuries, frequently changed but essentially the same. Rather, 'church' is something we choose to do or become, over and over, in constantly changing circumstances. Learning to become church is always a corporate task, in which some have particular roles on behalf of everyone; this local task is always truly undertaken in deliberate contact with those who have gone before us and those who are our contemporaries in differing situations.

There are many aspects to this venture and many participants, for example in thinking and experimenting with new forms of mission, worship, education, evangelism and the everyday following of Christian discipleship. These many insights have to be synthesized and chewed on to be digested and used for nourishing local church practice. Interwoven with ministry development, scriptural insights, the planning of mission and evangelism strategies and courses on clergy leadership, there is an important place for utter engagement with the love, tenderness and persistent desire of God for each one. The period from Ash Wednesday to Pentecost is an apt time for emphasizing this perspective.

There are many parts of this book that any Christian might want to use as material for personal reflection and prayer. Its main purpose, however, is to invite Christian communities of all kinds actively to enquire together how to become more a sign of God's compassionate and purposeful work in the world.

So here is both a warning and a challenge. The warning is that, unlike many books for Lent, this one can't be taken from the shelf and used as it stands. The challenge is that this is a deliberately worked example (through worship, scripture reading, silence, body awareness, and mutual witnessing) of learning together how more faithfully we can become 'church', in the circumstances in which we are placed.

This book's origins lie precisely in my own intention to make this way of church more possible through input and discussions I led during Lent, Holy Week and Easter 2005 in St Michael's College, Llandaff, the Parish of Neath and the Monmouth Group of Parishes. The material has been further tested and changed in use throughout the past year in the Parish of St Mary the Virgin, Monkseaton, Diocese of Newcastle.

- *Risking Everything* assumes a desire for corporate worship and learning.
- This could be of one or several congregations together; it could be ecumenical; it could be a group that exists or that is specially formed.
- Two or three people could absorb the material here in the months and weeks before Lent; this 'planning group' could decide how much of the learning and worship material to use and deliberately plan to include others in carrying it through.
- In this way the deep learning will be about both the aspiration and practice of a participative church and about an increased flourishing and drawing near to God for each Christian.
- Deliberately, I invite those who study these chapters to maintain their energy through Lent, Holy Week and Easter, all the way to Pentecost.

One of the reasons for flatness and lack of expectation in the mission of churches is the result of placing an overemphasis on being the Body of Christ, without also expecting to be the Temple of the Holy Spirit. Lent, Holy Week, Easter and Pentecost are a single movement. If we come to expect renewal throughout the whole liturgical cycle from Ash Wednesday to Pentecost, we shall see more clearly how it's only possible to continue the work of Christ through resting in the same Spirit that came down on him at the Jordan.

Many churches now are small in numbers and are composed largely of those of us in the second half of our lives. The temptation is merely to accept the comfort of familiar patterns of church life with people of a similar approach to life, omitting the urgent call of God that we should risk being more open to finding the desire and gentle confidence to reach out to others. Vulnerable churches have the advantage of knowing that hope lies entirely in accepting God's loving encouragement. Those rich in resources, buildings, money and personal energy have the harder task of letting go of their own successful planning and competence.

In first presenting some of these ideas within different groups my hope was that we might go beyond merely sharing words. I wanted to offer those present the chance to be as fully present to God and to each other as we might dare: in body, mind and spirit. Among those who first experienced this material, I shared my growing conviction that the churches are dying for lack of making true and honest connections with God, one another and society. In order to expect the sharing of personal insights, we agreed to commit to be present for each meeting: to assist the building up of community, to listen to one another with great care and to treat all that emerged with courtesy, sensitivity and confidentiality.

A key theme of this material is the gift and work of community inherent in Christian faith. To be in Christ as one, yet in kaleidoscopic difference, is not to choose a life of safety and self-protection. Rather the summons is to leave all, to obey and follow Christ in the risky way of self-giving, as partners with God in holding the world together. The practice of such discipleship will, of course, vary between each person and church community. I am working from the assumption that a core positive characteristic of church is a permanent attitude of dissatisfaction. How else shall we find urgency to discover new language, concepts, ideas or practical possibilities that emerge from responding to being embraced by God? The biblical themes of pilgrimage, journey, departure and arrival, of leaving and staying, are all invitations to consider what it means to be a mobilized, restless, apostolic community. How can Christian living be distinctive without becoming ghetto-like, and respectful of and open to all, without losing its character? These are perennial questions, as the church in every new time and moment learns to find its response to God's call.

Being real with one another

As the leader, I began by briefly reflecting on my own varied journey as a Christian disciple, as a spouse and parent, interwoven with 36 years of ordained ministry. In particular I appreciated how my vision and ideas have been stretched, encouraged and challenged through being married for over three decades to Claire. Having worked as a psychotherapist and supervisor of counsellors, Claire is now herself preparing for ordination. While recognizing just how important being a priest for over three and half decades has been to my own life journey, I placed a strong emphasis on the coming of the Holy Spirit, differently but equally, to each community and person in their vocations.

Others were then encouraged to speak briefly of their own sense of God accompanying or seeming absent in lives of many varying patterns. This happened in small groups of no more than three or four, though there was a chance for people to speak to the entire group afterwards, if they wished. Clearly this needs to be handled with care. The difficult but necessary task of leading these meetings will involve both drawing out the reticent and gently but firmly limiting those who frequently dominate but without being aware of the effect they are having. This applies to the leader too!

Practical arrangements

This book is composed of chapters with material which, if everyone has the book, can be read beforehand or in the group and then discussed. However, if only the leader has the book, a summary of the main points will have to be prepared in advance. It is suggested that the quotations and other material included should be offered as an essential part of the group meeting. Each chapter begins and concludes with suggestions for prayer and reflection. The later material for Holy Week is intended for those with responsibility for helping churches to plan worship and other events in order to continue the learning stimulated by the opening chapters and pointing us to Easter and beyond. Deliberately the material for the days in Holy Week often refers to the meaning and planning of events later in the week, which is an inevitable part of the journey together that this week can be.

A small planning group needs to consider well beforehand: is this event truly open to all those who might wish to attend? Is the room appropriate for the numbers expected? Is it warm enough, are the chairs suitable, is there access for people with disabilities? Is the space likely to encourage or restrict free discussion? Is there room both for meeting together and for breaking into smaller groups of three or four for more intimate conversation? Will there be opening and closing worship, and who will take responsibility for this? What atmosphere do we want to foster? Will it allow for participation by others? Will candles be lit? Will there be singing, possibly unaccompanied? Will there be music? Will printed sheets need to be prepared?

How will the material be presented? Will each person have a book or will someone summarize key points on a PowerPoint or flipchart presentation? How much of the available input will be helpful in a single session? Who will lead the sessions?

Will there be refreshments – before, during or afterwards? Will there be a clear expectation and welcome of newcomers? Will name badges help or be too formal? How will the sessions be advertised? Will there be a daytime and/or an evening chance to meet? How will the impetus be maintained later? What happens to the feedback from the groups? Other people's flipchart notes, however significant at the time, can be meaningless to others. Will the church council have a report of the meetings in the expectation of a response?

Acknowledgements

I would not have been able to write this book without the hospitality and inspiration of the spiritual guidance team at St Beuno's in North Wales, especially Fr Stanley Dye M.Afr. and Sr Perpetua Henry S.M. It also gives me great pleasure to record the formative influence of Phillip Morris, Ruth Moverley, Richard Pain, Stephen Ryan, Peter Sedgwick and Claire Greenwood. Many thanks also to Joanne Hill and members of the editorial team at SPCK for their careful editing of the final text.

The author and publisher acknowledge with thanks permission to reproduce the following material:

On pages 13–14, 'The journey' from *Dream Work* by Mary Oliver, 1986, Atlantic Monthly Press.

On page 38, 'Stanzas of the soul' from *The Collected Works of St John of the Cross*, translated by Kieran Kavanaugh and Otilio Rodriguez. Copyright © 1964, 1979, 1991 by Washington Province of Discalced Carmelites, ICS Publications, 2131 Lincoln Road N.E., Washington, DC, 20002-1199, USA. www.icspublications.org

On page 95, the prayer from *Eggs and Ashes: Practical and Liturgical Resources for Lent and Holy Week* by Ruth Burgess and Chris Polhill, 2005. Reproduced by permission of Wild Goose Publications.

1

A community of love

Welcome and opening worship

At the first meeting, the leader welcomes everyone (preferably individually as they arrive). As the meeting begins, the leader invites people briefly to move to greet anyone to whom they cannot put a name. It will be important to notice how some people have come from a busy day and that part of what they bring to the group is fatigue or anxiety. Also it will be a relief to some to know that they will not be made to feel guilty if, despite the ideal, they cannot attend each session.

A prayer, poem or song may be shared; there may be a reading from Scripture. For example, reflection on these words of the writer on contemplation, Thomas Merton, may lead into the adventure of this project:

> In the centre of one's nothingness, one meets the infinitely real. This act of total surrender is not merely a fantastic intellectual and mystical gamble; it is something much more serious. It is an act of love for this unseen person, who, in the very gift of love by which we surrender ourselves to his reality also makes his presence known to us. (*A Merton Reader*, p. 347)

How to respond to God's creative love

I recall talking in the pub with friends while I was at theological college in the 1960s. One said to me, 'The way I see it is that you've gone off to save your soul, so that you can learn to help us do the same.' This had echoes for me of Fyodor Dostoyevsky, in his *The Brothers Karamazov*, when he insists that nothing or nobody escapes the burning flame of God's love and that that is the heart of the life of the world. 'Were not our hearts burning within us?' the two disciples are reported by Luke to have said as they hurried back along the road from Emmaus to Jerusalem on the first Easter Day (Luke 24.32). Christians just assume that God is present to every person and situation, in darkness and light, recognized or not. The real issue is how to respond ever more fully, with gratitude, energy, penitence and hope, personally and communally, as well as becoming instrumental in companioning others in their engagement with God.

As a student, I heard an Ash Wednesday address by the New Testament scholar C. K. Barrett. He spoke arrestingly of the challenges ahead for those preparing for leadership in the churches. Unless we see ourselves as constantly on a journey of new discovery, consciously moving deeper into God, and as extraordinary when we discover our true selves, our ministries run the risk of becoming banal and our lives an irksome struggle.

Thinking and feeling

Looking back now, I believe our training for priesthood was overbalanced towards being head-centred. It's vital for all Christians to be rigorous on thinking about Christian faith and in teaching and preaching to take seriously the tools of historical and literary criticism. However, one of the things I have gradually been led to unlearn from my early experience of theological education is that knowledge and intelligence is not just centred in the brain and thinking. As I get older I realize more and more that having knowledge stored up in my head, however insightful, is but a small part of my true awareness or wisdom. The church cannot serve God's mission with full rapture when taking such a limited approach. The church fails its own people and clergy, as well as society, when it forgets how many different ways there are of people contributing to the store of knowledge, wisdom and flourishing.

Increasingly there are signs of churches truly wishing to encourage a wide variety of people to participate in liturgy, mission and ministry. There are many lively ways of being human and of contributing to community learning and living. In the local church, whatever its size or way of functioning, our task is to encourage one another in being open to the limitless blessings of God, growing up in Christ, with delight as well as with intensity, and so finding our place in sharing God's mission.

As a member of the Third Order of St Francis for a number of years, I've gradually come to realize how the Lord of all things can get under my skin and subvert my security when I'm off my guard or vulnerable. This can be especially the case when I take time to listen to the silence, draw, walk, laugh, play, gaze at a painting, or imagine myself in a Gospel incident. To begin to take God's word as my reference point is to recognize the whole of God's trinitarian life in the guts of God's creation. Not only that, but to avoid sentiment and simplicity is to lock up the gospel in mere words. In reality the practice of Christian faith is a total immersion in the whole of God in the whole of life for everyone, tracked through art, nature, poetry, drama, experiences joyful and painful, and never contained.

There is no 'either/or' between thinking and feeling; rather there is only becoming, with my whole being and all my gifts. When I let God break in to my entire life, suspicion of sentiment and feelings can be melted. God's goodness is all around and for us, showing us the deepest meaning of the life we live. We all have particular 'thin' places that talk to us, that are gifts to be taken into our hearts, where we can grow. Such a place for myself and for thousands of others, from across the world, is St Beuno's retreat centre in the Clwyd Valley. This centre for spirituality is a reminder of how every local church everywhere needs, in its own context, to be a crucible for imaginative prayer, study of Scripture and art, celebration of God's blessings, reflective worship, repentance and restoration, and for the development of Christian discipleship in ordinary living. Surrounded by hills, woods, streams, views of distant Snowdonia and of the sea, buzzards, crows, rabbits, mud, and amazing skies, it's a reminder of how when we experience deprivation, loneliness, fear, lack of direction or guilt, we can dare to open ourselves to new ways of moving on and growing deeper into God and into our humanity. On our life's journey we need constantly to review how at different stages we may need fresh resources and stimuli and to ask where we shall find what we need.

It's the most simple insight but fundamental, that wherever we are situated, we shall be miserable until we recognize with more assurance just how deeply we are loved by a compassionate God who offers us the terrifying invitation to be fully alive. Contemporary culture, illustrated by advertisements and chatshow role models, persuades us we are lovable only when we conform to certain outer images – thin bodies, this year's fashions, and the right glasses. Christian community living, instead, invites us to delight in the loving kindness of God supporting each person and to explore how this can be learnt through respecting the wisdom of our bodies and of the natural world.

This means taking time to become aware of our breathing, heartbeat, contact between our bodies and our surroundings, our feelings – are we driven or relaxed? – all as signs of our inner confidence and vitality. To what extent are we really present in and to our body, mind and spirit?

The Clwyd Valley was the inspiration for some of the poetry of Gerard Manley Hopkins, who trained as a Jesuit in the mid nineteenth century at what is now the St Beuno's Retreat Centre. One of his best loved poems, 'God's grandeur', well sums up God's often unacknowledged presence in the detail of life:

> The world is charged with the grandeur of God.
>   It will flame out, like shining from shook foil;
>   It gathers to a greatness, like the ooze of oil
> Crushed. Why do men then now not reck his rod?
> Generations have trod, have trod, have trod;
>   And all is seared with trade; bleared, smeared with toil;
>   And wears man's smudge and shares man's smell: the soil
> Is bare now, nor can foot feel, being shod.
>
> And for all this, nature is never spent;
>   There lives the dearest freshness deep down things;
> And though the last lights off the black West went
>   Oh, morning, at the brown brink eastward, springs –
> Because the Holy Ghost over the bent
>   World broods with warm breast and with ah! bright wings.

I'm a 'morning person'. My most receptive and productive time is early in the day. For me the morning is the time when I'm most likely to allow my mind and heart to focus on God. Yet I'm aware of how often I have missed the opportunity to listen to the Holy Spirit by letting the pressures of work deadlines rush me to my study or to a meeting and another hectic day.

As a priest, I've been especially fortunate in having been given so many resources, which are in fact needed by all reflective and growing Christians: frequent participation in Eucharist and other forms of worship, dedicated times of prayer, retreats, time set aside for Scripture reading, study, books, conferences, spiritual directors, a cell group, visits to churches in other parts of the world and people constantly praying for me.

The church has given all of us many milestones for praying alone or with others, chiefly in the daily offices and the Eucharist, but it's all too easy not to have an intimate relationship with the Lord, and it's possible for endless praying to make no real difference to how I experience myself, the decisions I make or how I relate to others.

There is an antidote to the church getting itself into a panic about survival, money, congregations, clergy, buildings, or even much discussed 'growth'. It is to make provision for the whole laity to be stretched and to overflow with faith, worship, prayer and the sense of serenity that evolves from true belief that, come what may, 'The Lord is here: his Spirit is with us'. A health warning should however be attached: an informed laity will no longer conform, accept worship without intimacy or be satisfied with being merely pew fodder.

Church as a crucible of God's love

The culture of the priority of the individual, rather than any group of which he or she is a part, unhelpfully encourages us to see ourselves as one alone, seeking to have our own needs met in the world and, worst of all, thinking we have to work hard to bring Christ to the centre of our lives. The world on those terms can be a very scary place and certainly not to be found in the New Testament. Writing to the Christians in Rome, Paul says that we are to know ourselves as 'in Christ', not that we are to struggle that somehow Christ may be in us. The Holy Spirit comes to energize us as the people of God for the task of practising faith for the world. The church is given to us as a community or a living space for learning first to receive and then to give love. We wouldn't be taking part in this meeting or reading this book if we weren't stirred by the possibility of living more closely in God's love. We may have all kinds of knowledge, perhaps sufficient wealth, but the greatest possibility for us is to be formed as the most authentic, true, human being God can make of us.

True wisdom is to know who we are with God, to be bodily alive and energetic, aware of, but not victim to, our wounds. Filled by the Spirit at baptism, we have the grace of knowing that we are deeply loved, home to the indwelling Trinity. Thinking and wrestling with ideas and practicalities are both vital parts of human and Christian work. They must not be separated from the challenge to open our hearts and feelings. Our calling is to commit ourselves to remain vulnerable, open to suffering, to risk coming out of our ego castles where we thought we could sort life out with our brains and will-power. Can we recognize this challenge to ourselves, to dare come out of our heads, where we justify, rationalize and defend our way of dealing with life and manipulating others to accept our picture of how things are or should be? Every Christian who chooses to discover their true potential for life, joy and the flourishing of their unmasked self should consider asking someone, lay or ordained, to act as a soul friend or spiritual guide.

Every human person lives with the dangers of becoming self-important, fearful, vain, greedy for human respect. These are all the symptoms of a self that is anxious, demanding and deceptive. Psychologists tell us that living in authoritarian and hierarchical patterns of church actually makes impossible the very gospel patterns of living we advocate. Top-down patterns of church encourage us to become childish, in destructive ways, to develop a spirit of competition and rivalry, jealousy, the search for status, something for nothing, and the privileges of being one up on others. We all live with a sense of shame – not just guilt about past wrongdoing, but a deep sense of uneasiness or unworthiness. 'Why has God called me?' 'I'm an impostor if only people knew it.' Jesus invites us instead to dare to recognize how deeply God loves us. If our life within the church compounds rather than alleviates this, we can be worse off than before.

Taking support

A simple spiritual exercise to help us know this consists of three actions:

The first is to stand with feet slightly apart and hands by our sides, imagining the whole company of all who have gone before in the handing on of faith – whoever comes randomly to mind: Abraham, Sarah, Amos, Deborah, Elizabeth, John the Baptizer, Mary, Joseph, Mark, Joanna, Paul, and so on through the saints till now. Let them into your consciousness with thanks.

Second, reaching your hand above your head draw down into yourself the presence of Christ, the power of the Spirit, the love of the Father, the protection of the angels, the life of all churches throughout the world. Feel their vibrating presence accessible to your life now.

And then, third, move your arms around you, noticing the space and the possibility of contact with others. This space is the uniqueness of your life, the unique place that is your gift from God, to be and grow, to know, feel and grow. It's a territory to guard from destructive invasion by others, so that you know who you are but equally it's a habitation from which to set out with openness, resilience and love to work with others for the completion of love in the world.

The purpose of the regular use of this exercise is to grow in the desire and possibility of becoming vulnerable, real, authentic and able to know the truth about our real motives, fears and terrors. Jacob, awed after his dream about the ladder to heaven with angels of God ascending and descending, said, 'This is none other than the house of God and the gate of heaven' (Genesis 28.17). There at Bethel he set up a rock, anointed with oil, as a testimony. Experiencing the awesome presence of God, if we would know it, is the only place for church communities to build foundations for mission.

The false self

One way in which some have come to understand the fight within each of us is through the language of a 'true' and 'false' self. To live in the false self is to identify ourselves by putting ultimate trust in success, work status, possessions, or the opinion of others about us. The Jewish and Christian traditions often speak of faith as setting out on a journey. The purpose of setting out is to take leave of the ego, or tyrannizing false self, and increasingly place our trust in God. When we are trying to grow beyond the things we dislike about ourselves – resentment, cynicism, fear, jealousy, lack of real contact with others, low self-esteem – we are seeking our true heart, our true self. The true self is what we call wholeness, the ability to know inner peace in the midst of outer turmoil, healing of past hurts, the ability to give to others, and above all a commitment to the journey to life in its fullness.

At some stage in our childhood, or maybe later, we began to cope with difficulties in relating to others by living in an adapted, defensive life of pretence. It started simply as our way of dealing with the imperfections of our families, our schooling and with the beliefs we inherited. The combined effect of this was to lay on us quantities of guilt, fear and shame. The resulting mix of learnt prejudices, taboos and anxieties, often leading to neuroses and imbalances, needs to become the raw material for conversations with Jesus. If we truly believe God cares for the very hairs of our heads and knew us as we were formed in the womb, we can engage in intimate conversation in which God can help us to see these prejudices for what they are: obstacles on our journey.

Called by the Spirit, each one of us, in our given difference, shares in Christ's ministry. However, our work and our lives can become limited and impoverished. Easily we can become prey to depression and emptiness when our true self remains damaged and hidden deep within us. In turn this closes us in on ourselves so we are even less open to others reaching out to embrace us.

How are we to be healed and no longer be controlled by the ego? How do we breathe life again into our lost, true self? Are we even aware of the ego, so clever and plausible are its persuasions, so totally in control does it grow within us so that we are no longer real? Communities rooted in God's love are the place to crack the shell of my control, for new life to break from deep within.

Most of the wise ones who have looked at these issues over long periods agree that to reach an appropriate maturity and responsible individuality, we must learn to observe ourselves and so learn how to distinguish our egotism from our true self. We start this process by keeping a vigilant and detailed watch over the arrogance and self-righteousness of the ego. We have to remember that the ego is not entirely a negative force. It has been shaped as a protection, through our efforts to cope and find a safe place from which to survive. It is fundamentally a positive, creative energy of the Holy Spirit. Its task is to be a reliable companion and friend. Christian worship and life together offer us resources to tame the tyrannical ego and to bring to life the co-creator ego. There is no denying the difficult journey; that's why we must take support.

Giving up the struggle

Rembrandt's depiction of the powerful story of the return of the prodigal son may prove helpful in nourishing our imagination to get in touch with God's deep love. With the help of the reflections on this theme by Henri J. M. Nouwen, we can enter into the experience of the younger son who leaves his father's home. This was no gap year or cultural world tour. The younger son deliberately anticipated his father's death by demanding his inheritance now. He despised, rejected and left his father's 'home' – physically, intellectually and emotionally, searching for love, meaning, salvation where it could not be found.

Then one day, in desperation and with limited hope, he arises from the pigsty. He chooses to leave the foreign country, electing to end his state of rebellion, closing the era in which he has allowed himself to be diminished. With humility he moves back towards home but with as yet no real hope of how he might be received. Amazingly his rehearsed words of confession are muted by his father's touch of blessing. All that he had to do was admit he had been wrong. He knows now he is unable to make it on his own. Instead of the hired servant treatment he would have given himself, the father invites him with dignity to reclaim his place at home. A second innocence is given him.

This raises questions for us now: are we struggling still to make our lives work through our own limited insight, energy and inspiration? Are we still resisting the father's embrace? Would we rather be treated as a hired servant, with no responsibilities? Do we want to be a true son or daughter, surrendering ourselves so fully to God's amazing love that a new person can emerge?

All that is important about the journey home is that we begin it. That beginning calls for courage. And staying with it calls for courage too. It is God who does the transforming; all we have to do is stand up and start walking. Silently, invisibly, we are purified. In the walking we become more alert, relaxed, leaner, looser. As we put down old assumptions, we see things more clearly. And the more we empty ourselves of what before seemed so important for our survival, the more room there is for God to become our energy. The miracle is possible that gradually we can allow God to free us from the dark places and grandiose illusions that have ruled our life.

Allowing God to embrace us

Whatever arrests our imagination will determine everything through each day: from rising in the morning, choosing how we spend our time, what we read, what we are amazed by, what fills us with pain or with thanksgiving. It's a matter of where our love is centred – that will decide everything else.

St Augustine describes the journey into the self as the journey home to God. Two questions you may like to ponder are: 'Do you feel you are called out on a special journey by God?' If the answer is 'Yes', the second question is: 'Have you the courage, trust and the support to begin?'

Mary Oliver encapsulates something of the drama and the excitement of setting off on a journey to live only by God's love for us:

One day you finally knew
what you had to do, and began,
though the voices around you
kept shouting
their bad advice –
though the whole house
began to tremble and you felt the old tug
at your ankles.

It was already late
enough, and a wild night,
and the road full of fallen
branches and stones.
But little by little,
as you left their voices behind,
the stars began to burn
through the sheets of cloud,
and there was a new voice,
which you slowly
recognized as your own,
that kept you company
as you strode deeper and deeper

into the world,
determined to do
the only thing you could do –
determined to save
the only life you could save.
            ('The journey')

Becoming a community of love

Christian discipleship is always corporate, yet we damage it through our lack of love for God, for ourselves and for others. I know how easily I am offended. The love we learn in Christian community is tough, requiring a disciplined approach. To love others is essentially to believe that God is present in both them, and ourselves, equally.

There is no room for a rescuing, altruistic, patronizing approach. In a trinitarian community of love, in all our separate and different identities we are one. Mutuality is the key. We become ourselves in loving others. The calling we share is to reach out to another, clearly and insistently. We vary in our capacity to love others, but with as much consistency as we can command, our believing in the other can summon them to a fuller, more reflective life, give them the courage to mature, to take a new step, to abandon their sense of hopelessness, and draw them out of the shell into which they had retired. We need each other to teach us that we are capable of showing humility, kindness, affection and vulnerability. It's never a one-way process, though at different stages of life our capacity to be loved and loving will vary.

The return of the prodigal son invites us to recognize that a fully mature Christian will have learnt how to be at times the younger son or daughter returning, at others the older son or daughter, called to be accepting, and eventually to become the father or mother who welcomes with joy.

Witnessing to one another in small groups

Psalm 59.17 speaks of God as the strength of the believer, a fortress and one who shows steadfast love. In small groups of three or four at the most (to allow for intimacy and sufficient time for each to speak) try some of the following:

- When have you experienced really good trusting love from another person or group?
- Tell a story about someone you have known who showed what love can be.
- Recall a time when you showed costly love to someone else.
- Describe an experience when you felt held and loved by God.
- How is Christian love making a particular contribution to the neighbourhood and wider world through our performance of the faith? What more is possible?

Closing worship

A form of night prayer could be used and, if praying with others, include several voices. Psalm 121 would be appropriate and this prayer of Ignatius Loyola could provide a conclusion:

Take, Lord, and receive all my liberty, my memory, my understanding, and my entire will, all I have and call my own. You have given all to me. To you, Lord, I return it. Everything is yours. Do with it what you will. Give me only your love and your grace, that is enough for me.

(quoted in Harter, 2005)

2

A community of abundance

―――•◦•―――

Welcome and opening worship

Choose prayers, readings, poems, songs on the theme of abundance, gratitude and self-giving to help you engage with this theme.

Part of Psalm 27 may be helpful, or this prayer of St Francis of Assisi:

> You are the holy Lord God; who does wonderful things.
> You are strong; you are great; you are the Most High.
> You are the almighty King.
> You, holy Father, King of heaven and earth.
>
> You are three and one, the Lord God of gods;
> You are the good, all good, the highest good, Lord God,
> living and true.
>
> You are love, charity; you are wisdom, you are humility,
> You are patience, you are beauty, you are meekness,
> you are security, you are rest.
>
> You are gladness and joy, you are our hope, you are justice,
> You are moderation, you are all our riches to sufficiency.
>
> You are beauty, you are meekness,
> You are the protector, you are our custodian and defender.
>
> You are our strength, you are refreshment. You are our hope,
> You are our faith, you are our charity.

You are all our sweetness, you are our eternal life:
Great and wonderful Lord, Almighty God, Merciful Saviour.

Exercise in self-awareness

The abundance of God's overflowing blessings is often overlooked. To be aware of and grateful for all that we are and have is the beginning of new life. (If you are doing this alone, start at 'Sit and relax'.)

The leader invites everyone to find a settled position and then to take time to be aware of:

Those here now – can you name everyone? If not, introduce yourself and exchange names.

Your body and its environment:

Sit and relax. Take a little time to pay attention to your breathing and heartbeat. Try to become more aware of your body. Notice the sensation in the different parts. Can you experience your feet on the floor, your feet inside your shoes, your clothes against your skin, your back against the chair? Is your jaw locked tight? What about your hands? Go round and visit each part in turn. Do you have pain anywhere? Notice where it is and where it is not. What can you see around you: a chair, a person, a door, a piano, a window, a tree?

Listen to your heart. What feelings are you aware of at this time? Stress, anxiety, uncertainty, rawness, anger, happiness, peacefulness? Does one stand out? Are you holding this in a part of your body? Where exactly? What is your dominant feeling at this moment?

Recall those people you have been with or aware of today – face to face, on the television, by telephone, or

---

17

through e-mail or letter. How conscious have you been of God at work in the networks of communication?

Using this process on your own at other times will allow you to expand the amount of time given to each element and to develop the process that will be most helpful to yourself. Through today and the next few days, gently bring your mind back to your body, along these lines. Experiment by noticing your feet on the ground, your feet in your shoes, the touch of your clothes, your back on the chair, any aches and pains, what you see as you let your eyes move around, briefly noticing one thing after another. Gradually through this practice you will experience a new steadiness, relaxation and ease about you. You will sit, stand, move and breathe with more grace, confidence and vitality.

Learning to observe ourselves

Earlier, we explored how an essential antidote to living in the false self is to begin to grow in self-awareness and awareness of our surroundings. I have found that this takes courage and persistent fresh starts, and is in fact a lifetime's work.

What keeps me open to the possibility of making progress in this way is the clear idea that an unreflective life is no life at all. God invites us to live in the sacrament of each present moment, rather than being obsessed by the past or gripped by visions for the future. We can be transformed from our egocentrism if we're willing to give careful attention to each present moment, an awareness of what is happening now, and now and now: all that is happening in my head, heart and body, and around me, as the day goes on. What a difference to relationships, families, churches, communities and nations it would make, if we gave this even a small amount of our energy.

The Greek word *chronos* speaks of time passing, while *kairos* is about the urgency of each moment – now! It's time! Time's up! There is a sacred and unique timelessness (*kairos*) to each moment (*chronos*). Suppose we begin to train ourselves to be alive to every present moment, finding the presence of God in the apparently mundane.

Jesus shows us the amazing blessings God wants us to receive

The whole of Jesus' ministry is an apocalypse or dramatic breaking in of the overwhelming generosity and overflowing love of God towards creation. The wedding at Cana recorded in John 2.1–11 provides a stunning example, demanding a response of faith. In rescuing a family from shame, Jesus shows the amazing abundance of God's providence.

John describes the events at Cana as the first of Jesus' 'signs' and so it stands at the start of his ministry as a foretaste of what is to follow. Each jar held two to three 'measures' – around 150 gallons, or 800 bottles of best-quality wine, at the end of a long celebration. Such stories of amazing amounts of wine, corn and oil are to be found elsewhere in the Bible – the roots of Christian praise and thanksgiving for God's wonders lie in the Old Testament accounts of a God of superabundance, energy, and awesomeness.

John's Gospel is saying, 'The hope of God's people of a future of fulfilment for all is like a great wedding banquet; then all will be satisfied. It's begun already: here in the ministry of Jesus of Nazareth, so make up your minds to recognize him as God's expected Son – for that is who he is.'

Remembering abundance

In small groups of no more than three or four, or on your own:

- Remember as many of the healing miracles and sayings of Jesus as you can. For example, the healing of Simon's mother-in-law (Mark 1.29–31) or 'Give and it will be given to you. A good measure, pressed down, shaken together, running over, will be put into your lap; for the measure you give will be the measure you get back' (Luke 6.38). There are many other testimonies in Jesus' ministry to the generous blessings of God.
- Discuss how you experience God's gifts and life at work in you.
- Think of examples from your experience of Jesus' principle that we live by giving life away.

The leader draws everyone together again to hear a few examples of stories and ideas from the groups.

Communion

Koinonia is a key New Testament word, used to speak about Christian 'communion', 'communication', 'community' or 'a people filled with the Holy Spirit'. It's a deep Christian principle that the journey of faith is to allow ourselves gradually to be drawn into sharing in the common life of the Holy Trinity, Father, Son and Holy Spirit.

At our baptism our name becomes forever connected with Jesus' name, our life linked with the crucified. Baptism is to become part of Christ's life, death, resurrection and ascension. As he was called and empowered by the Spirit and is now available to us in every time and place, we are called to know the same Spirit at work in us, enabling us to continue Christ's work. It's a huge responsibility to take our share in doing the will of the Father. It requires putting down, bit by bit, all our damaged and demanding parts. It is only possible to the extent we know in our guts how much we are deeply loved by God.

The work of the church

The following may be starting points for further thinking, feeling and conversation. What attitudes, hopes and practical outcomes might emerge in the particular situation in which your church is set?

Church exists for mission as does a fire for burning.
From your experience of reading and hearing Scripture, how are God's people compelled to engage with the world in social justice, seeking righteous relationships and evangelism?

Church as body of Christ.
If through God's Spirit we are the Risen Christ in the world, what demands does that make on us?

Church as participation in the Trinity.
God is a community of three in one, where each finds who they are through the others. To echo this life in church and world, what kind of community will the church be? How will it act?

Ministry as radical discipleship.
Consider the extent to which your church takes risks and faces uncertainties to bring about the transformation of the world.

Church as formative faith community.
What is distinctive about this community? How are we built up in love?

Many different pathways to a common end.

A Trinity-shaped church has no problem with including many different people and cultures. How is it that so few differences are apparent?

Closing prayers

Use a form of night prayer and end with the following:

> God our friend, you never change,
> you are always there for us.
> We thank you that when we are lonely or helpless you watch over us.
> Hear us,
> be with us, as you were with your Son,
> alone on his cross.
>
> (adapted from *A New Zealand Prayer Book*, page 609)

3

A community of integrity

Welcome and opening worship

A song, reading, silence, or an object or picture placed centrally may be ways into this reflection.

> May God who has anointed us by baptism into the church
> pour upon us the riches of his grace,
> that within the company of Christ's pilgrim people,
> his anointing spirit may daily renew us,
> and come to the inheritance of the saints in glory. Amen.

Summarizing earlier themes

In what we have considered in the two chapters so far, what stands out, puzzles, annoys or intrigues you? (In a group the leader will be able to draw out comments and make connections in whatever way seems helpful.)

Testing our powers of observation

When any insights have been shared and possibly written on a flipchart, the leader asks everyone to stand and face the same way – perhaps looking outside the building or at some part of the inside. If everyone looks the same way for a minute and is then asked to answer simple

---

questions on the detail, the results will be amazing. Try it together: how many trees? What colour is the wall? How many chairs? What colour are the curtains? Were there flowers? If so what kind? And so on. Different witnesses will see the same event and disagree on the 'truth'.

(If you are doing this alone compare your attempt at recalling the scene outside your window with the reality a few minutes later.)

We tend to believe what we want to believe. In life generally, what doesn't fit with our expectation we try to ignore. We exclude certain people: Jews, travellers, gays, asylum-seekers; anyone who spoils our picture of a settled life for ourselves.

As part of the new task of observing ourselves introduced earlier, we can develop the practice of recognizing how we limit our observation and start really listening. Resolving to make a start and checking ourselves means the journey has begun.

Authenticity, truth, integrity, freedom

Christian community living is essentially a deliberate enactment of the truth and meaning we find in God. It is a coming together of people who choose to shape their common life as a disciplined and exuberant expression of the good news. In the gospel of Jesus, the truth and freedom to be found in God combine. Jesus said that the integrity of the church will be apparent in its fruits (Matthew 7.16) and that when we live the truth we are made free (John 8.32).

What could it mean to be a community of those who do the truth and enjoy freedom? What do we mean by a free person? It is someone who is not copying someone else but finding an inner integrity, motivation or confidence. Teachers of the type of prayer that leads to human maturity suggest that it is only when I have learnt – or rather am learning – to become aware of my breathing, befriend the way I feel just at this moment, however confused or damaged, and allow my feelings to have a voice, only then that I begin to know what it might be to live with integrity, to act 'from within'. Once we find this path, freedom becomes possible within us, as part of our growing character, as an experience of ourselves, an inner joy and peace. Communities of truth have at least a few members who are on the way to this freedom that (truly self-) controls and results in a tranquillity that surpasses all suffering. In my experience truly free people are rare. I see that as a challenge rather than a reason for despair.

The medieval Persian prophet Rumi invites us, in his poem 'The Waterwheel', to 'stay here, quivering with each moment like a drop of mercury'. The teacher of prayer Anthony de Mello insists that the present moment is the only truth but it takes patient discipline to reach it. It takes a growing self-awareness and demands not less than everything. Ordinary looking is all that's needed, but in a way that is increasingly consistent, present and relaxed.

In the last chapter (pages 17–18) I offered an exercise in self-awareness. Let this become part of the routine of your prayer life. As a reminder, here it is again (to be used either alone or as a group experience). You may want to keep referring back to this until you have adapted the process to your own particular rhythm and needs.

Exercise in self-awareness
- Put down any books or papers and sit with both feet firmly on the floor, hands on top of thighs. Sit and relax. Pay attention to your breathing. Try to become

---

more aware of your body. Notice the sensation in the different parts.

- Can you experience your feet on the floor, your feet inside your shoes, your clothes against your skin, your back against the chair? Is your jaw locked tight? What about your hands? Go round and visit each part in turn.
- Do you have pain anywhere? Notice where it is and where it is not. What can you see around you: a chair, a person, a door, a piano, a window, a tree?
- What feelings are you aware of at this time? Stress, anxiety, anger, happiness, peacefulness? Does one stand out?
- Are you holding this in a part of your body? Where exactly? What is your dominant feeling at this moment?
- Recall those people you have been with or aware of today – face to face, on the television, by telephone, or through e-mail or letter. How conscious have you been of God at work in the networks of communication?

Developing self-awareness

Becoming a fully alive and reflective human person is not a given but a lifetime's work. St John invites us to dwell in God's word, but usually we prefer to learn the world's message about ourselves and others. So we define ourselves by our past mistakes or achievements, squashing ourselves completely or inflating our pride; we define ourselves by what we do for a living, how others appreciate us or by what we own. We ignore the truth so often repeated in Christian worship: that the power for transformation lies beyond our own strength, but is the one great gift that God constantly invites us to receive. Only this knowledge, settled deep into our personality, rescues us from trying to live by pleasing others or by projecting on to others all our own fears and self-anger.

Here we need to reinforce the earlier theme of self-awareness. I am grateful particularly to my wife, Claire, who has worked to integrate Christian spirituality with the theory and practice of gestalt psychotherapy. Eastern teachers on prayer have taught me the importance of awareness of my breathing and heartbeat, without attempting to modify their rhythms. We mostly take them for granted. Holistic growing and spiritual mindfulness requires that we seek the transformation of our consciousness. Deeper than changing behaviour, this leads to an integrated sense of our whole being, more than understanding or knowledge, more than a deep grasp and perception of body, mind, spirit.

It springs from and is developed by a spirit of worship. Through a sense of awe the psalmist wrote, 'For it was you who formed my inward parts; you knit me together in my mother's womb. I praise you, for I am fearfully and wonderfully made. Wonderful are your works: that I know very well' (Psalm 139.13–14).

Spiritual exercise

In various strands of the Christian tradition there is a pattern of blessing our body for its demanding journey, by making the sign of the cross. It can become a powerful ritual so long as it remains a mindful act. Carefully we trace the sign of the symbol of God's overcoming death or evil across our mind, body and heart. We place ourselves once more under the protection of the Trinity, of the Creator and Sustainer of Life, of the Saviour of Humanity, of the Spirit of Love. As an act of faithful courage

---

we touch the forehead and chest. In the Eastern tradition this is to open up the brow and the heart as centres of vision and compassion.

Further, according to Jewish wisdom, as we briefly but definitely touch the left and right shoulders, we are activating the spiritual focuses of mercy and strength. I immediately find here a helpful connection with Paul's helmet of salvation and Patrick's breastplate. To arise deliberately each morning within the strengthening protection of the Trinity can, I find, be a huge encouragement, especially when the day is due to bring difficult challenges.

How do you respond to this? Why not try it out over the next 30 days and then reflect on the experience?

Developing awareness of the mind

The art of conscious living, 'mindfulness', is an attentiveness that is refined and attuned through prayer. The opposite of just letting things go by is a trinitarian recognition of the interconnectedness of everyone and everything, and the rich possibilities that arise from this. It is the remedy for tunnel vision and personal bias or prejudice. It's about daring to live really or authentically. We do this through beginning to spot each time when we have gone into our defensive castle or hidden behind a mask, a convenient lie, sarcasm or cynicism, a pretence, all the defences we learnt a long time ago to protect our ego. So this journey is not a country ramble with no end in view; it's a deliberate and dangerous climb, requiring patience, perseverance and a vision to help us beyond distractions. It's a journey not to be attempted alone but through the help of friends, spiritual companions, retreats, cell groups, reading, and the sustained practice of prayer. One spiritual leader expresses it in these terms:

> By being with yourself, by watching yourself in your daily life with alert interest, with the intention to understand rather than to judge, in full acceptance of whatever may emerge, because it is there, you encourage the deep to come to the surface, and enrich your life and consciousness with its captive energies. This is the great work of awareness; it removes obstacles and releases energies by understanding the nature of life and mind.
>
> (Maharay, 1992, p. 10)

Centring prayer

There are so many ways of praying. In the group you may be able to talk about the various experiences, the new starts and stops members have known. Between us we've tried a great variety of ways of praying and may well go on all our days exploring new pathways. We know how many of the lifelong saints, monks and mystics died believing themselves to be beginners in the life of prayer. A bishop said to me once, 'Youthful energy will take you through till you're forty, but then what?' The second half of life is not really a continuation of the first. Carl Jung claimed that what supported us in the morning of our journey will be insufficient to sustain us through the afternoon.

As we've noticed already, to be this kind of totally relaxed eternal self-watcher, reflector or timeless witness, requires attention to how we breathe. If it is to become second nature, our prayer will be the training ground. We all have different lives, relationships, spiritualities and there can be no prescriptive answer that suits everyone. The Eucharist, daily office, Scripture, praise, penitence and intercession are vital ingredients of the church's ways of praying. However, to change our deeper life some dedicated time each day, perhaps using a word from

Scripture, the Jesus prayer – 'Lord Jesus Christ have mercy on me a sinner' (or a shortened version) – or a story from Scripture in which we can centre our imagination, seems essential.

We die to the false self by the practice of prayer. I am grateful to the writings of Thomas Keating and M. Basil Pennington for introducing me to very personal ways of listening to the word of God.

A simple form of 'centring prayer' involves four steps. Its purpose is to acknowledge that only by surrendering and allowing God to be the centre of our being can we make the deep transformational changes for which we long.

The first step is to be still and offer our 10 or 15 minutes of prayer to God, using the body and breathing awareness exercises, perhaps making the sign of the cross or saying a familiar prayer.

Second, we choose a word that stands out from careful reading of a passage from the Bible – or we may have a word that we use over a period of time, such as Father, Love, Mercy, Peace, or whatever becomes important for us.

Third, we remain in stillness and when a thought comes along we gently push it away with our chosen word – but we don't use the word as a mantra to be recited all the time.

Last, when the pre-selected amount of time for prayer is ended, we use a familiar prayer and perhaps sign ourself in blessing.

In such prayer our desire is not to change anything, but to notice, without altering, our breathing, letting God fill us at very deep levels and transforming our tormented selves. You may say, 'I haven't time'. I won't be surprised. I often tell myself the same.

Becoming real

We all have certain obstacles to face. We must confront our lack of attention and weakness of will, our attachment to our cherished opinions, slavery to our likes and dislikes, and our perpetual fear of loss. All of these characteristics form the main material for the work of transformation, to be transformed by allowing God's love to get through our clever and persistent defences. It is necessary to awaken to this self, which has the power of love that can melt away the false self, the ego.

All of us, as God's people, are at different times participants and leaders in the church. Acknowledging our ordinariness is an important but sometimes difficult step. I know how years of 'church speak' as a public minister can dull me to the immediate and surprising presence of God or separate me from the summons to be as a little child. We all face temptations, trials and negative feelings which God can transcend.

The liberation of Christian community is to know that we do not remain victims of our own and other people's egos, hopelessly stuck in closed, self-destructive cycles. A real danger, and one of the greatest inhibitors of church growth, is that many churches do not allow this level of awareness to blossom. The church can be just as formal, stuck and imprisoning as any other organization. If that were not sad enough, we have all experienced at times in other organizations that which we long for and desire particularly within the church.

Letting God be in charge is the key that opens the door, though we may fear putting down our familiar masks and ways of coping. Allowing ourselves to be the returning prodigal son or daughter gives us the freedom to know our need and to find our peace. There is no need to pretend to a virtue or ability to change things that we do not have. If we could just be, we would be able to relax from the anxiety of becoming something we are not, getting something we don't have and trying to force reality into the shape of our own desires. And yet what we most need is what God has already made us. Instead of running away, we could just come home.

Small group or individual work

- Read the Beatitudes (Matthew 5.1–11 and 2 Corinthians 3.17f.).
- What could that mean in practice for you and this church community?
- Were you clear about centring prayer? Could you imagine using it each day – where and how? If not, what prayer is already serving the same purpose of helping you to know your authentic self?

The art of reflection

In his book *The Heart's Journey Home*, Nicholas Harnan offers four ways of promoting the art of reflective living:

1 Slow down; cultivate a slower rhythm in your daily life.
2 Reconnect with a deeper order in reality, an order beyond your immediate control.

3 Stay with an experience in order to discern its deeper meaning and resist all urges to try to manipulate it.
4 Share your thoughts and feelings with a trusted companion.

Closing worship

At the close of this meeting, the leader or another may pray for a deepening awareness of God's presence walking beside us and that we will have the courage to slow down and be emptied out the better to know this gift. A form of night prayer or a penitential service might be used. You may want to include some singing and other suitable prayers or readings.

4

A community of learning

━━━━◆◆◆━━━━

Welcome and opening worship

O Spirit of God
We ask you to help orientate
all our actions by your inspirations,
carry them on by your gracious assistance,
that every prayer and work of ours
may always begin from you
and through you be happily ended.

(a prayer frequently used to begin Jesuit meetings)

Revisit the awareness exercise outlined on pages 17 and 25.
Read and reflect together on this story:

Once when Francis fell ill during his last years, his guardian
and companion obtained a piece of soft animal skin to sew
into his tunic as protection against the winter cold. Francis
would permit the soft skin liner only if a piece were also
sewn on the outside of his tunic so that no one would be
fooled by the garment's coarse outer appearance into thinking that Francis was being more ascetic than he actually was.

Relate this to your own life or the life of your church.
As a group or on your own you may pray in your own
words, ending with the Lord's Prayer.

Learning by and from all

In a church community no one is exclusively a teacher or a learner. Everyone brings a contribution to the learning of all. A simple test of the truth of this claim is for the leader to ask everyone to prepare for this session by writing down five questions from their particular area of expertise in life. As most other people fail to answer the questions correctly, everyone is shown to have a unique knowledge, which added to the pool makes for a rich community of learning.

Living with ambiguity

Knowing and accepting the truth about ourselves is tough work. Today is an invitation to bring us to our selves, to break through a little more into a greater sense of our authentic or real authority as people called to be friends of God. We've seen how our ego can be either constructive or destructive, a friend or a tyrant. A devious and false sense of who we are can fill our lives and blunt our work through inner suffering, anxiety and fear. A spiritual guide writes this:

> So long as we haven't unmasked the ego, it continues to hoodwink us, like a sleazy politician endlessly parading bogus promises, or a lawyer constantly inventing ingenious lies and defences or a talk show host pouring out suave and emptily convincing chatter, which actually tells us nothing worthwhile. To end the bizarre tyranny of the ego is why we go on the spiritual journey, but the resourcefulness of ego is almost infinite and it can at every stage sabotage and pervert our desire to be free of it.   (Rinpoche, 1992, p. 117)

Small group or individual work

One way we can tell we are on the road to recovery is how we react to criticism or rejection.

In a spirit of confidentiality, in groups of just two or three, share an experience when you have felt deeply criticized. How did you react at the time? What is your reflection on it now?

It will probably not be appropriate for details to be shared outside the small group. However, general points may be offered to the wider group, at the leader's discretion.

Being ordinary

We need not be shocked by what we find going on inside ourselves. We are not angels, neither are we demons. There is a kind of suppression, in childhood, of the dark dimension of our psyche, which in later years wreaks havoc with our sanity and peace of mind. There is a divine spark and a powerful evil in all of us. And they are closely intertwined. You cannot pull out the badness, leaving the goodness intact, any more than you can pull out weeds without damaging healthy plants. As Alexander Solzhenitsyn wrote:

> If only it were all so simple! If only there were evil people some-
> where insidiously committing evil deeds, and it were necessary
> only to separate them from the rest of us and destroy them.
> But the dividing line between good and evil cuts through the
> heart of every human being. And who is willing to destroy even
> a piece of his own heart?   (*The Gulag Archipelago*)

Becoming more aware of the power of each decision to move from preoccupation with ourselves to acting with love for God is liberating, a passover, or bridge from the false self to the authentic person we are called to be.

Letting Jesus heal us

'Who are you?' Jesus invites us not to define ourselves as either successes or failures. Rather, God is to be our reference point. In the light of God's saving work in Christ we are already a new creation. This gives us a confident and safe place to explore how we may increasingly let God's kingdom be born in us. Learning does not come easily to our false self. It cannot bear to be wrong and rushes into denial, defence, self-pity. We need to notice, too, our reaction to praise, to being top, to being proved right. Our wrestling is to notice the danger of defining ourselves only in terms of achievements, possessions or popular approval – or the opposite – only through the eyes of others, dependent on their verdict. So we have no inner centre, no grounded self. Our journey of bodily and mindful awareness is about becoming less self-centred, less touchy and prickly, less gullible and fearful. Becoming aware, without judging, is the vital first stage.

Jesus experienced negative feelings – doubt, disappointment, fear, hunger – so it's likely we shall never be free of them. The task is to be more and more aware of our response. Are we working with Jesus to allow them to be transformed? Letting go is a kind of dying, being emptied. God in Jesus came as a defenceless baby; he was stripped and crucified. He shows what love is: letting go for the sake of the immense reward of transfiguring life. At baptism we all had the seed of Christ sown in our hearts. Seeds grow in hidden darkness; so we can be transformed into the life of Christ – by letting go.

Mystics such as St John of the Cross push us to stop wrestling with our shame and difficulties and to let ourselves be taken over as in a love affair with God.

One dark night,
fired with love's urgent longings
– ah, the sheer grace! –
I went out unseen,
My house being now all stilled.

In darkness, and secure,
by the secret ladder, disguised,
– ah, the sheer grace! –
in darkness and concealment,
my house being now all stilled.

On that glad night,
in secret, for no one saw me,
nor did I look at anything,
with no other light to guide
than the one that burned in my heart.

This guided me
more surely than the light of noon
to where he was awaiting me
– him I knew so well –
There in a place where no one appeared.

O guiding night!
O night more lovely than the dawn!
O night that has united
the Lover with his beloved,
transforming the beloved in her Lover . . .

Upon my flowering breast
which I kept wholly for him alone,
there he lay sleeping,
and I caressing him
there in a breeze from the fanning cedars.

When the breeze blew from the turret,
as I parted his hair,

it wounded my neck
with its gentle hand
suspending all my senses.

I abandoned myself and forgot myself,
laying my face on my Beloved;
all things ceased; I went out from myself
leaving my cares
forgotten among the lilies.

There is nothing we can do. The only power we have is the power to resist God from finding, loving and taking us over. The greatest temptation is to not let God be God and so we have to become God ourselves. But God is endlessly persistent.

Reflect on your own life story alone or in the group. Can you trace God's loving pursuit of you? How do you resist being found?

Deep empowerment comes when we consciously let go. God's invitation to be part of his kingdom, reign, loving kindness and good news for the world is demanding yet unbelievably healing and life-giving. Despite our massive resistances, we are as human beings deeply designed precisely for this kind of growing. Jesus died many deaths before his final agony.

Earlier I mentioned with affection C. K. Barrett. He reminded us of John Wesley's hope for each human being that we would have the liberating experience of letting go, being converted, followed by the journey to holiness that is the rest of our lives.

Experience tells us that the task of allowing ourselves to be transformed is never completed. Nor is it easy as our pride and false self stand in the way. We are filled with contradictions and paradoxes. It is, in fact, about loving our enemies, cherishing our wounds, celebrating the very things that trip us up, slow us down, block our path, frustrate and frighten us. Without these things happening or dark memories, there can be no healing, growing or travelling. Our best learning comes through what we may regard as our enemy or thorn in the flesh. Jesus asks us to love our enemy. Paul believes that, 'All things, even sin, work together for the good of them that love God.'

Down the centuries Christians have spoken of experiencing God as light in darkness, goodness in the midst of tragedy, gift in a time of loss, life when faced with death, heaven among the dust or ordinariness. God is there for me and for all people.

One experience of a rescuer on the day of the London Underground bombings (7 July 2005) recounted the appalling sights in the wrecked carriage and the amazing possibility of 'doing your job' in a crisis only because of previous and life-giving experiences of being human, having a friend or receiving a hug (*Guardian*, 9 July 2005).

The examen

Learning disciples need to find some anchor or simple structure, such as the examen of consciousness. I am indebted to the St Beuno community for my introduction to this way of reviewing what has been happening in my life and what God is asking of me now. I'm still learning to have the courage and humility to know God's unconditional love to be able to give it the attention it deserves. There are a variety of descriptions of this reflective process, all of which emphasize the need to rely on the Holy Spirit to release us from whatever hinders our journey to wholeness. Here is one:

1 **Act of presence**
Jesus, I know that I am in your presence. You are the Way, the Truth and the Life. I believe that you come with your vision of faith, so that I may be able to find God in the events of this day. Count me among those who do not see, and yet believe.

2 **A petition for light, wisdom and acceptance**
Jesus, please give me your gift of light so that I may see clearly, your gift of wisdom to understand what I see, and your gift of acceptance to receive humbly and gratefully what I come to understand.

3 **Examination with thanksgiving and/or sorrow**
Jesus, together we let the events of today pass before us, like a train moving past . . . When you bring something to my attention, help me to stop, and let my comfortableness or uncomfortableness show how I have used God's gifts of creation, and how I have responded to God's building of the kingdom . . . Thank you where I have responded well; this is God's gift. I am sorry where I have responded poorly. Help me to distinguish true guilt from false guilt, and to increase in self-knowledge and self-acceptance.

4 **Request for help tomorrow**
Jesus, come and be a real part of the coming day. Help me grow into the fullness of my humanity by growing into you. In particular tomorrow, Jesus, help me live according to my deep desire to . . . Especially help me in regard to the obstacle . . . Thank you, Jesus; thank you, God, source of all life, and Holy Spirit. In you and in your love all is gift.

By keeping the mirror of awareness clear, we can begin to free ourselves of our compulsions and inappropriate thoughts and behaviour. Awareness is the means; the present moment is the focus.

Soon after the death of Rabbi Moshe, Rabbi Mendel of Kotzk asked one of his disciples: 'What was most important to your teacher?' The disciple thought and then replied, 'Whatever he happened to be doing at that moment.' Why not start again now? What baggage will we let go of today, this Lent?

Spiritual exercises

1 Plan a daily meditation on something you have observed about yourself that you want to move on from. Begin by focusing on the negative emotion, deliberately letting go of it with every outgoing breath.

2 Spend time observing your breathing and being aware of your body and your surroundings. Now bring into awareness a person or situation that gives you pain, drawing an imaginary circle of light around them. Gradually through God's love growing in us, we let negative feelings fall away; we reflect on the benefits this person or place has brought to us. There is nothing we cannot do when we're empowered by the Holy Spirit. So we bless this person, releasing them from our anger, and we pray for our next encounter.

3 Imagine yourself as a boat with a sail, filled with the wind of the Spirit. Paul said: 'I can do all things in him who makes me strong.'

Courage

Recognizing our woundedness and frailty opens us to expect God to act for us and Jesus to be at our shoulder. Instead of words of justification and bravado, I am coming to recognize how much transformational power lies in our bodies. Facing a new day with all its unknown as well as already known challenges, St Patrick's Breastplate, combined with the signing of my body with the cross, provides words of blessing that are filled with potency:

> I arise today through a mighty strength, the strength of the Trinity, of Christ's resurrection, of love, of nature, of God's creative, self-starting power.

Working in Christ for the world

If the church is a learning community for the sake of the world, the role of the ordained and others in public ministry is to assist that learning. We must begin with ourselves and our own need to be honest about our lack of hope that Christ is being formed in us.

Discipleship for each one begins from learning from the gentleness of Christ that we are infinitely and unendingly loved, blessed and forgiven. We will always be the returning younger son on the long way home, or like Nicodemus, invited to see and work for the kingdom through being born from above. Also we need to recognize part of us as always the elder brother, unable to conquer the darkness of jealousy from our side, needing the leap of faith to believe the father loves us too, so that we can reach out easily to embrace our returning brother. Learning how much I am myself loved, I am also invited finally, as I grow older and hopefully humbler, to take on the role of the father. We are eager to be called minister, vicar or father and offered respect in church leadership, whatever our gender. We look forward to or enjoy the responsibilities and pleasures of public ministry but for this we have to be growing into fatherhood and motherhood. Compassion is the quality we need for this.

This includes grief, forgiveness and generosity. We grieve and mourn for the world's tragedies and the human beings placed in our charge; we learn the way of unconditional forgiveness that has to overlook our sense of being wronged; and we learn that generosity of which Jesus spoke when he said, 'No one can have greater love than to lay down our life for our friends.'

To be open to this gift, as we saw earlier, is to have the willingness to recover from our damaged egos through grace. The father of the two sons is always calling us to new levels of self-acceptance, to gently break the patterns of insecurity and fear that feed our habits of jealousy, criticism and blame. We must attend to ourselves – become aware, minute by minute, of our body, mind and spirit and to monitor our own transformation.

To be father, mother, daughter, son, sister, brother, or grandparent is to be part of a web of belonging. Our hope of salvation is within the ordering of people in families, neighbourhoods, societies and globally. As leaders in the church, the greatest accomplishment for which we can hope will be to reach out our hands to embrace those who still prefer to live in a far country, and to know that we can accomplish this only through the immensity of God's unfailing love. In God's new ordering of life, shown to us in Jesus by the Spirit, the only rule is that of love. We shall only be able to serve this new order in our hearts, minds and bodies if we allow ourselves to be embraced again and again by the Father whose flexible ordering invites us to lose ourselves and be shaped by his indestructible love and overflowing joy.

Small group or individual work

- Consider how babies learn their earliest sounds and then begin to connect them with real things.
- Consider how small children learn that they are loved and what damage takes place when they don't have that primal experience.
- Consider how belonging to a church has helped you to learn more about being loved and how to love others more.
- Notice the different ways currently offered to church members for learning faith and love. What is missing? How could you make a difference?

Closing worship

An Awareness Examen at the End of the Day

We pray that the Holy Spirit will help us to review our day in the light of the gospel . . .

1 What of today's events can I recognize as a gift from God?
2 Reflecting on Romans 7.15–20, where was I working with, and where against, God's love?
3 I allow myself to receive forgiveness for the times when I ignored God's active presence with me.
4 I look ahead, asking God's Spirit to walk with me in all the situations that tomorrow will bring.

Concluding with:

> Batter my heart, three person'd God; for you
> As yet but knocke, breathe, shine and seeke to mend;
> That I may rise, and stand, o'erthrow mee, and bend
> Your force, to breake, blowe, burn and make me new.
> (John Donne)

5

A community of character

─•◆•─

Welcome and opening worship

Everything given to Christ is given to the church.

(John 17.7–8)

The church is sent into the world. (John 16.7–24)

As Jesus performs God's life, so the church performs Christ:

Let nothing hinder us,
Nothing separate us,
Nothing come between us.

Wherever we are, in every place,
at every hour, at every time of day,
every day and continually,
let us all truly and humbly believe,
hold in our heart and love, honour, adore, serve,
praise and bless, glorify and exalt, magnify and give thanks
to the Most High and Supreme Eternal God, Trinity and
Unity,
Father, Son and Holy Spirit,
Creator of all,
Saviour of all who believe and hope in Him and love Him,
who, without beginning and end, is unchangeable,
invisible, indescribable, ineffable, incomprehensible,
unfathomable,

blessed, praiseworthy, glorious, exalted, sublime, most high,
gentle, loveable, delightful,
and totally desirable above all else,
for ever, Amen.

(St Francis of Assisi)

Reflection

So far we have reflected on church as a community of love, abundance, integrity and learning. This has involved an ongoing theme of welcome, embrace, and the acceptance of difference in relation. Consider for a few moments what has been important for you.

Activity for a group

The chairs are in a circle or an arc, leaving a space in the centre. The leader asks everyone to stand. In a humorous way everyone is invited to form a line to show:

- How long have you lived here? (some interesting negotiation required)
- How many years have you been part of a church?
- How many years have you been with the church you go to now?

Notice how it may be the clergy who have been here the shortest time. What conversation and insights arise from this activity?

Who are you? Where do you come from? Are you one of us?

The leader provokes a discussion (if you are reading this alone reflect on your own experiences) on the question of being different from those around you.

Consider times when you have been a stranger or visitor, times when you have noticed foreigners having trouble getting what they needed, times when you or others felt excluded – in the family, in school, in the neighbourhood or church.

Bring to mind those who live locally who prefer things different from you and your friends or church, e.g. music, food, clothes or attitudes. How do you react to or reach out to such different people? Do you feel a gap between them and yourself?

We have considered the church's task as agent of God's kingdom and sign of all that God wants for creation. What urgent implications does this have for dealing with those we see as different?

Religious groups have been as likely as others to become shut in their own culture: the former Yugoslavia; ethnic, cultural communities; holy murderers defending the Christian faith against Muslim intruders; or consider Ireland, or Palestine.

A key invitation from Jesus is to become a salty community: 'If the salt has lost its saltiness, how can you season it?' (Mark 9.50). 'It is no longer good for anything, but is thrown out and trampled underfoot' (Matthew 5.13).

He invites us to repent precisely by letting God's kingdom come near, in us – and so resisting being caught and self-satisfied within our own culture, in blind self-righteousness, for instance against asylum-seekers, travellers, gays, blacks . . . and sharing God's hope for all people, seeking to have *both* a proper appreciation of *and* a suspicion of our own culture – a critical distance in the name of Christ.

Abraham

Consider the story of Abraham. He has become a towering figure in the foundations of Christian faith; as Paul says, 'the ancestor of all who believe' (Romans 4.11).

Abraham believed in the Lord (Genesis 15.6) that he would have an heir – and became 'the father of us all' (Romans 4.16) – and this belief becomes the foundation of the faithful life of the Jewish nation. Abraham heard God's call to go out from his comfortable home, family, culture – to become great – to be a blessing to all families on earth. He must depart and cut all ties, not knowing where he is going (Hebrews 11.8). The one God has a single message for all nations – a voyage, a journey, an exodus, being a stranger, is to be a child of Abraham and Sarah. They and their family left their settled and known place, native country to stand at the beginning of a new history of a pilgrim people, the body of the Jewish nation.

Readiness to set out on a journey, trusting only in God, is an essential part of Christian identity – for communities and personally.

The witness of Paul

Paul's writings are the earliest accounts we have of Christian faith in practice. An enthusiastic first-century Jewish believer, a Roman citizen, a Hebrew scholar, Saul of Tarsus, walks down the road with a troubled mind. The Torah, the law, claims to be the text of the one True God of all the world but it has become narrowly focused on just one nation, almost one family.

He was shocked into a new understanding as God broke into his life, so that for three days he was physically blind. Baptized by Ananias, he perceives God has spoken a new word to him:

1 Though still important, the law is not necessary for membership in the covenant with God.
2 The promise made to Abraham, which he believed, was not about racial purity but about faith and grace. The family tree and genealogy are not enough. What God has done in Jesus is available to all who believe it (Romans 4.11–12).
3 Paul embraces Christ, crucified and risen, the seed of Abraham, in whom there is no longer Jew or Greek, slave or free, male or female (Galatians 3.28). In Christ all the families of the earth are blessed on equal terms by being brought into the promised single family of Abraham.

Paul sees that just when Abraham was at a dead end he responded to God's call to a new commitment. So Paul recognizes God's offer of faith to all humanity. Faith is not mere trust, or even the will to believe, or the commitment of myself to Christ. It is simply the discovery that God has made us righteous in the work of Jesus Christ. What Jesus did is made actual in us. From the beginning this meant belonging to the group of those who know they are recipients of God's work in Christ. And the mark of this group is baptism.

Baptism in the Spirit replaces all other groups – gender, race, wealth, status, tribal allegiance. We are immersed in the running water of the Spirit, drowned into life in Christ, transforming our minds and our allegiances. Water (being in Christ) is thicker than blood (my family).

In baptism we are signed with the sign of the cross, branded with Jesus' name and vision. The cross gives us a renewed identity. Through our receiving the self-giving of God, we are able to imagine offering self-giving life to others.

Baptism creates a people as the differentiated body of Christ; just as one loaf of bread is made from many grains and now broken for all to share it, we have many different members. Against all culturally conditioned expectations God invites us into communion, not hierarchy, in radical equality – women and men – celebrating all our different ways of seeing, thinking, feeling and talking.

Departing while remaining

Part of our Christian character is to know that here we have no abiding home. Through the Holy Spirit we share in the joy of Jesus Christ which is the love of the Father, exploding within us. We are in the world but not of it.

Down the ages for many this has meant the call to the desert or the monastery. Is there anyone in the group who has ever considered such a calling to religious community? What awareness have you of the many varied possibilities – contemplative, missionary or working for justice and peace?

For most of us this call means seeing ever more clearly how to live in and transform our world, as disciples, neither ignoring our own culture nor being overawed by it. The Third Order of St Francis offers a growing number of Christians a structured support and corporate reflection for following a vocation in the world of work. The danger for Christian churches lies in becoming ghettos of worshippers but outsiders to the very place where God has put them.

In the group or alone ponder

- How responding to the call of the gospel means one foot in and one out.
- A sense of distance and of belonging.
- Being at home yet as strangers.
- Not inheriting the 'land' (Genesis) but the 'world' (Romans).
- To depart without leaving – allegiance to God but here and now.
- Evil that cannot be tolerated.
- Constant observing, judging, choosing, wrestling.
- To be shaped by the gospel, attempting to reshape the world.
- Engaged in a battle against evil in the world, in our own culture.
- Racism – how to be multicultural and hold our faith while respecting others.
- Listening to Christians from other cultures when they visit us . . . and vice versa.
- How can we be ready to ask 'Is this war just?' What oppression should we be against? Who should we be protecting?
- Where can we use our influence for the work of Christ?

Closing prayers

Read together the Beatitudes (Matthew 5.1–16). Invite members of the group to pray for the church and current sharp issues of human exclusion in the world, as a response to each line:

The poor: the kingdom of heaven is theirs.
The gentle: they will inherit the earth.
Those who weep now: they will be comforted.
Those who hunger and thirst now: they will be satisfied.
The merciful: they will be shown mercy.
The pure hearts: they will see God.
The peacemakers: they will be called children of God.
The persecuted: the kingdom of heaven is theirs.

Conclude by saying slowly the Lord's Prayer and, signing yourself with the cross of God's blessing on your body, say the Grace.

6

Holy Week

———— ·•·• ————

As the introduction to this book made clear, all the material here is offered ideally as a working resource for parishes wanting to use the Lent–Pentecost period as a deliberate further development collaborative ministry. The material for Holy Week offered here in no way supplants the church's liturgies. Rather it is presented as an amplification of or supplement to the regular worship of Holy Week: introduction, material for confession, addresses, discussions or intercession, during or after a celebration of the Eucharist or other form of worship. Use as much or as little as is appropriate in any situation. If your parish hasn't already considered it, this is one of the best times to initiate a worship or liturgy group in which a small group in partnership with any licensed ministers can take responsibility for looking ahead and drawing in others to be creative with each act of worship.

Palm Sunday

This is a day for all ages together to be helped not to see ourselves as indifferent spectators but to pray with imagination as committed participants. Together we have to face the truth that we 'hand over' Jesus not just in shouting 'Hosanna' through worship, evangelization and witness but in betrayal, demanding that he be crucified. As we act out this day the level of our commitment to Christ may rise to trouble our hearts. Are we happy to stand with one who will be condemned to death by the authorities and powers?

However few in number – and why can't churches very close together make this a joint service? – we need to have an outdoor procession, to carry a palm and sing praise to Christ our King. So people should gather a few minutes before the usual time for the morning service, in a hall, school – a couple of stewards could welcome and make sure people know what's happening. Children may have been helped to make banners in preceding weeks to increase the sense of festivity. Rather than keeping all the crosses together before the service, distribute them as people arrive. To be given them ceremonially by the clergy and servers gives off a very different message about power and everyone's involvement. The choir or just two good voices might well sing a lively song of praise to welcome the Son of David to call everyone to alertness. The priest or presiding minister speaks informally but with urgency about the benefits of joining in the events of Holy Week, and says a prayer of gathering and blessing, sprinkling the palm crosses and people with holy water (however your tradition understands that expression). In a few concise sentences the congregation's hearts are warmed to praise Christ and receive him again as king. There follows the invitation to process, as did the Jerusalem crowd, in welcome of Christ.

The choir and everyone join in a favourite hymn of praise to Christ the King. The cross, decorated in celebration, banners, thurifer (if that's your style), red vestments, lead the celebration. The repetition, year in, year out, of a once exciting event that has become moribund is sure way to kill off interest and hope in this week. A worship group should have the freedom to be creative, with the prime concern to release everyone to celebrate. Different well-known hymns that people know almost by heart could be used. In a sizeable church the choir may be most effective halfway through a procession rather than at the front or back. Once in church, the organ can pick up any lack of confidence in the singing.

The mood should be quickly felt to change, however, as the readings turn to the passion. In the passion reading everyone needs a copy with their parts highlighted, including the crowds. The passion mood now prevails through the service. A brief homily is essential to articulate the moment and encourage people to be caught up in the transformative drama of Holy Week.

Monday

The readings

Some or all of the readings from the lectionary may be used and introduced at the opening of the worship.

Isaiah 42.1–9: The call to be a servant, to work for justice, to open the eyes of the blind, to know ourselves as prisoners released from the dungeon.
Psalm 36.5–11: 'For with you is the fountain of life: in your light we see light.'
Hebrews 9.11–15: Christ as mediator of a new covenant.
John 12.1–11: Mary anoints Jesus' feet; the chief priests' plot.

Welcome and introduction to worship

During the three days following Palm Sunday, Jesus lived in the village of Bethany, near Jerusalem. He visited the city each day, teaching and talking to the people who gathered in the outer courtyard of the temple. We can consider ourselves as a temporary community – learning from Christ – in which everyone counts. We encourage each other by travelling together – not just individuals who happen to come, thinking we won't be missed . . .

We are part of the worldwide family of Christians keeping this solemn week. Imagine people all over the world, observing Holy Week as an event, expecting God to be with us, begging God to give us the grace to let go, to be freed, to allow God to fill us and to become the centre of our lives.

Promise of personal and community growth

This is a week for renewing our relationship with God. As far as we can we should put aside all other commitments. It is a time for reflection:

- We all need staging posts in life to stop and take stock.
- Holy Week offers a chance to dare to look inside our lives, to see ourselves more as God does – to know that we are deeply loved and to know we are invited to discern God's will for us and have courage to follow it.

At its heart is a three-day cycle: Good Friday, Saturday, and Sunday – the map of God's salvation: death, loss and new life. Making each day count in a different way is the church's offering to us and the world to help us receive into ourselves the capacity to know God in tragedy, absence and triumph.

God's calling to us

The cross lies at the heart of Christian life. It is the key to reading all that Jesus Christ did in his life. This week we consider again the meaning of the cross and its consequences for how we live with one another.

Jesus comes this week to the cross, neither by accident nor with outrage. The cross is the necessary outcome of his entire mission. The sufferings of Christ on the cross are not just his sufferings. The image Jesus left to the world, the cross, is the proof that God cares about all suffering and pain. His sufferings on the cross are the sufferings of the poor and the weak, which he shares in his own body and in his own soul, in solidarity with humanity. Since God was in Christ, through his passion Christ brings into the history of this world's pain the entire life of God. On the cross Christ shows that God is with those who are victims of violence, illness and being crushed in whatever ways. They are put under God's protection and given that which has been taken from them.

In traditional Christian speech we say that the cross is God's atonement for sin, injustice and violence on earth. Traditionally when we say 'God', we are referring to the communion of relationship we call the Trinity. Between Father, Son and Spirit exists a self-giving, a self-surrender, reciprocal relationship, mutual vulnerability – in short, 'love'. God's love, the watermark in the whole of creation, is about two things: first, a giving away for others, for enemies, for sinners; second, the inviting and drawing in of all who respond or believe to the life of God.

So God offers to all the love of which they have been deprived in one way or another – through abandonment, abuse, bereavement, exclusion or hatred. God will not abandon anyone but wants to include everyone in the communion of love. Fundamental to the gospel is the affirmation that on the cross Christ 'died for the ungodly' (Romans 5.6). When we struggle, suffer or are harassed or helpless we can find comfort in God in Christ being at one with us.

Are we humble enough to open ourselves to receive and to pass on this reconciliation?

We show that we have received this good news by living the same pattern of self-giving as Jesus himself. Jesus lived in close attention to Abba, his Father. He taught his disciples to pray to be part of God's kingdom coming on earth as in heaven. To be a disciple is to live the same pattern of obedience as Jesus' loving care for his followers. Yet we and the whole of humanity and creation are constantly breaking communion with God and with one another; our natural tendency is to hurt rather than to bless and live for one another. In human life, normally, the shepherd deserts the sheep and the wolf eats the lamb – we are called to a new world, one that only God can make with and for us.

Christian communities that are growing in maturity recognize the cross as the end of blaming others. When things are changing and uncertain (inevitable marks of a church that's risking letting God be at work), it is natural to pass on our fears and anxieties to clergy and others who are leaders or who will listen. The important challenge is for us to check ourselves from making scapegoats of others. Rather than passing on the fear, we need Christ's help to hold it, absorb it and let ourselves be changed. This is the time for the whole congregation to be challenged to pray for the Spirit's protection and guidance to know the best way forward that will carry as many different people as can be.

Being aware of prisoners

For this reflection it is helpful to have a very visible pile of chains as a focus for the eye. Have some candles ready to light and a bowl of sand.

We are becoming prisoners of our own fear. At their best, communities pride themselves on old habits of hospitality to strangers, the open door, the accepting heart, and welcome. One of the selfish reasons for welcoming strangers was that it meant a time to rest from work and an excuse to feast.

There is a sense today that we don't know who our enemies are or how to recognize them. Instead of a ready welcome to the stranger we erect barriers and are wary. We teach our children the habits of avoiding the stranger. Traditional hospitality and trust have broken down in the face of waves of asylum-seekers said to be threatening to engulf us. We are afraid of foreigners and travellers and of those who are different. We may wish to aid Africa in order to ensure that out of despair they do not become our avenger.

Within our society record numbers of people are in prison, while suicides in prison have reached a national crisis of huge proportions. There is a common view among many that the prison population should be reduced, that putting people in prison is not the best way to reconcile their lives or to restore society. There are increasing moves to bring new hope to prisoners through art, music and imagination. There have been successful attempts to offer retreats transforming lives in prison.

Yet the prison population continues to rise rapidly. In Britain in 2005 there were approximately 73,000 people in prison; by the year 2010 the prison population is likely to be 110,000.

In a group or alone consider
- Instead of banishing troublemakers from society, what would God have us do?
- Supposing we thought about the reconciliation of society with the one proviso that locking people away

---

is not usually the best option. How would that alter the outcome?

- We may count ourselves among that part of society that works hard and tries to be honest. We can be impatient with those who make a great mess of their lives. How can this week take us deeper?

- How can we hear Jesus' demand that we visit the prisoners – in every sense of that word – as part of our response to our salvation and God's call to us as a community of welcome and hope?

Ourselves in chains

It's hard but possible to bring ourselves to think about others as prisoners; but Holy Week is an important opportunity for us to think of what binds *us*. Jesus came to give us life in all its fullness, to live in God's word to us: 'You are mine and I have called you by name and I love you.' Dare we look into our hearts and ask how we are prisoners, living only half a life, trapped by old memories, broken relationships, illness or fear? Isaiah promises that our God will take us by the hand and release us from prison, from sitting in darkness . . . behold I declare a new thing, says the Lord (see Isaiah 43.19).

Do we want God's offer, or shall we leave it for some other time? Will we say, 'No, let some other person have it, but really, Lord, I'm OK, I can manage, I don't need your freedom. Honestly, I'm doing fine. What, trouble, sadness? Well, you know, just a bit, like anyone, but I really don't want to think about it . . . Look at the new lambs and the daffodils, it'll soon be Easter.'

Imagine yourself in chains and Jesus now standing beside you, perhaps placing his hand on your shoulder, inviting you with his eyes to accept his offer of freedom. God has done the work in Jesus.

Access that power to overcome . . . Sit with your eyes closed, relax your body, and say over and over to yourself the phrase, 'I am precious in your sight and you love me.' Picture the chains and think about the particular way in which you feel imprisoned in your life, asking God for the miracle of freedom from . . . and to . . .

Feel free to light a candle and place it in the sand to pray for your chains to be taken away and to pray for all prisoners and for one another in this temporary community of Holy Week.

Tuesday

Some or all of the readings from the lectionary may be used and introduced at the opening of the worship.

Isaiah 49.1–7: I was named in my mother's womb to bring God's people back to him.

Psalm 71.1–14: You are a rock of refuge; my praise is continually of you.

1 Corinthians 1.18–31: God destroys the wisdom of the wise; the true nature of God's strength; God chose what is despised.

John 12.20–36: We wish to see Jesus; a grain of wheat must die; we are children of light.

Welcome and introduction to worship

Jesus, through the Spirit, promises to us personally and as community, endlessly fresh, new and abandoned life. This is a week for renewing our relationship with God. Today our focus is on finding peace with God, with ourselves and with one another, daring ourselves to look inside, dive deeper into God. Recall how we are choosing to support one another this week by becoming a temporary community.

The theme today is God's good news of hope and mercy, for all the places where we – and the world – need healing. If we are celebrating the Eucharist tonight it will take the form of a service of penance.

God's calling to us

The cross lies at the heart of Christian life. The image Jesus left with the world, the cross, is the proof that God cares about our suffering and pain. He died of it. He invites and empowers us to become cross-shaped – cruciform. This is not a burdensome task but about being conformed in the renewing of our minds; to become cross-shaped is a gift, given to each of us in baptism. A key part of the baptism service is to receive the mark of the cross. Like the Eucharist itself this is a reminder and a giving of God's self-forgetting abundance, distributed among us.

Baptized and baptizing communities turn everything upside down – the early Christians were said to be turning the world upside down – by imitating the giving away of love. Before we do this we need to allow God to turn us upside down. Many churches are built in the cross shape to remind us to dream of and work for a world shaped on the cross.

Francis often prayed with arms outstretched. We are all cross-bearers, drawn into a way of life rooted in self-denial, as

63

a willing sign of hope in the world. So with arms outstretched
let us keep a silence.

Looking on the figure of the crucified with arms
outstretched, let us pray to the Lord . . .

Silence

> Most High and glorious God,
> Enlighten the darkness of our hearts
> and give us a true faith, a certain hope
> and a perfect love.
> Give us a sense of the divine
> and knowledge of yourself,
> So that we may do everything
> in fulfilment of your holy will;
> Through Jesus Christ our Lord
> May the life-giving cross be the source of all our joy and
> peace. Amen.   (St Francis)

God on the cross

Luther said, 'The cross is planted ever anew wherever existence
is threatened.' Many words have been used to try to explain
how God, the infinite Lord, is on the cross, goodness in such
an abysmal event – how can it be? How can it make a difference to us?

Many people do not come to church because they think it's
a place to be told off, or because there is so much evil in the
world. But this is precisely what church is for, to help us deal
with the real evil in ourselves and in society and in the way we
relate to creation.

In John's Gospel a group of women keep vigil, standing
firm in the face of fear, grief and the scattering of most of the
other disciples. Standing by the cross Mary and John are turned

towards each other by Jesus' words and given into each other's care (John 19.26–27). They represent the new community of true believers that Jesus came to establish. Beholding each other in a new relationship, the mother of Jesus and the beloved disciple mark the birth of the new family of faith founded on the commission of Jesus to bring all people into the same holiness and unity in the Spirit, shared between God the Father and the Son (John 17.4 and 21).

This new family, the church, will have the key characteristic of mutuality. Mary and John are shown as equal partners within the fold of the Good Shepherd. This mother and this son, Mary and John, are symbols of a larger group, the church.

When we experience ourselves as bound and locked in, God brings freedom and forgiveness. Christ bears and does what we ourselves cannot do. We misunderstand when we forget that sin is all about relationships and how we ruin and corrupt them or cannot bear them. When our relationships get too difficult we often sever them, but God in Jesus says, 'I love you so much I'm willing to bear you, stay with you, see this through.' What we have to face this week is our human condition. Separately and together as a human race we do terrible things to one another. Jesus on the cross brings about reconciliation. In him we can forgive and be forgiven. In forgiving me Jesus bears the suffering rather than writing me off. This is God's work. The cost of forgiving is to stay with us, to bear with us and the world, despite all the terrible sin of which we are a part, both in ourselves and as part of society. The cross is where God's forgiveness and the cost of that forgiving show.

Prayer of St John of the Ladder

A seventh-century monk on Sinai expresses our sorrow for sins as though we were the man who fell among thieves and

was rescued by the Good Samaritan, Christ himself. This is a
meditation on today's Gospel reading.

> I have become, O Christ,
> Like the man who fell
> Into the hands of robbers
> And was left half dead by their blows.
> So I have been wounded,
> Saviour, by my own sins.
>
> Travelling on life's way, O Christ,
> I have been severely injured by thieves
> Because of my passions.
> But raise me up, I pray.
>
> My passions have stripped me
> Of your commandments,
> Christ my saviour,
> And I have been injured by my pleasures.
> But pour your mercy on me.
>
> When the priest and Levite saw me
> It was clear they could not help
> For they passed me by.
> But you in your mercy
> Have now given me salvation
> And brought me to safety.
>
> My restless thoughts
> Have robbed my mind.
> They have wounded me
> By my passions
> And left me for dead
> In my many sins.
> But Saviour, heal me.
>
> By my thievish thoughts,
> O Saviour, I have ruined my life,
> Beaten by my sins.

So I have been stripped,
O God, of your divine image,
You who love humankind.
But have mercy on me.

Come, let us work in the vineyard of the spirit
And make the fruits of repentance grow in it:
Not working hard for food and drink,
But by prayer and fasting
Bringing virtues to perfection.
Then the lord of the vineyard will be pleased
And will provide the wage
By which he redeems us from the debt of sin
He who alone is merciful.

Examination of conscience

So we move towards repenting the wrongs we have done:

The worship leader in his or her own words leads people into penitence.

Water placed in a suitable bowl can be a reminder of the calling and the cross-shaped character we were given at baptism. What are the things we want to repent of? How do we want to be changed in response to God searching us out today? You may want to allow people to spend time in silence or listening to music; people may want to bless themselves or one another with the water.

Suggested song: 'Spirit of the living God'

(*Repeat song using 'us' rather than 'me'*)

Absolution (in words of the leader's choosing)

The Eucharist continues as appointed for this day in Holy Week.

Wednesday

Some or all of the readings from the lectionary may be used and introduced at the opening of the worship.

Isaiah 50.4–9a: I gave my back to those who struck me; he who vindicates me is near.

Psalm 70: O Lord, make haste to help me; O Lord, do not delay.

Hebrews 12.1–3: Jesus, pioneer and perfecter, endured the cross, disregarding its shame.

John 13.21–32: Judas betrays; God has been glorified in Jesus.

Welcome and opening worship

The theme of today's reflections is penitence out of love for God who has come close to us in love.

Recall the theme of Holy Week as an event and ourselves as community.

This is a time for growth. How am I stretching?

What do I want? 'Ask and it shall be given.'

A Taizé chant, such as 'In the Lord I'll be ever thankful', could be sung here for a while.

Prayer

Father,
In your plan of salvation
your son Jesus Christ accepted the cross
and freed us from the power of sin and death.
May we come to share the glory of his resurrection,
for he lives and reigns with you and the Holy Spirit.
One God, for ever and ever.

Looking to tomorrow

Tomorrow we shall be commemorating the final supper Jesus shared with his friends and the agonizing watch in the garden of Gethsemane before the soldiers came through the olive groves in the dark to arrest Jesus. It's a chance to learn to pray again.

What is the meaning of Passover for our lives today?

The main key to understanding Jesus is that, in common with his Jewish people, he knew that God is lovingly involved in every detail of life as well as in the broad sweeps of life's journey. In the freedom from oppression, exodus, the desert journey, Moses' covenant, the prophets, John the Baptizer, Jesus' life and ministry, communication with God in prayer was central. Reflect on God as protector and sustainer of all life. This is the theme of the Passover focused in the image of the angel overshadowing God's people in Egypt.

Silent prayer vigil

Later we shall have a silent prayer vigil. For some this will be attractive and helpful but for others a matter for anxiety. 'How can I be quiet? What shall I do?'

In the pace of the original events of Holy Week we follow through the actions and words of Jesus.

Participation

Early Christians coined phrases to describe themselves, such as the body of Christ, a vine and its branches, treasure of the kingdom, citizens of heaven. They recognized that sharing the good news as those who have been baptized and especially in times of trouble and affliction is always a corporate experience. In Christ we are never alone.

Imitation

As disciples we are in a relationship of formation. Paul encourages his churches to 'become imitators of me as I am of Christ'; to be 'in Christ' implies the obligation to follow his teaching and example and also knowing that we are uniquely gifted. The most obvious practical example of how we grow through imitation is of following Jesus' relationship with the Father in prayer. Imitating Christ in prayer leads to knowing most profoundly the openness, trust and dependence that are characteristics of a life of participation in God. This is the key to Jesus' and our own life. It's a well-tested principle that we become the God we contemplate.

Spending time contemplating an icon of the Trinity may well be helpful at this point.

Recall Jesus' own experience of prayer during his baptism by John. He knows himself as:

– the specially favoured son of God on whom the dove descends, thrust out into the wilderness to find his real identity, commissioned to bring God's good news close to others;
– intensely in conflict with evil precisely because of his close familial intimacy with the father.

Consider how you are also chosen, invited to know yourself and your vocation and sustained by a close relationship with God.

Prayer as Jesus' constant pattern of life

Jesus selects his disciples after spending a night in prayer. He thanks God for the mission of the 70. The transfiguration happens in the context of prayer. He teaches people to pray, repeatedly. He prays for his disciples in lonely spots on mountains or in the garden of Gethsemane. He prays in the temple. He shares in Jewish festivals. At Passover he joins in singing the Hallel (Psalms 116–118). He uses the daily *shema* (Hear, O Israel, Deuteronomy 6.5ff.). Familiarity with the synagogue prayers is very apparent in some of his teaching.

Jesus commends persistent personal prayer for healing and deliverance; for strength to carry on; for confidence as a person rooted in relationship with God as Father.

From the centrality of Jesus' relationship with God arose his deep conviction that all the circumstances of life, history and even nature were subject to the unstoppable advance of the kingdom of God. People came to recognize the extraordinary power and authority that arose from Jesus' prayer life: 'only speak the word and my servant will be healed' (words of the Capernaum centurion, Matthew 8.5–13). He encourages disciples to claim this for themselves and takes it for granted that they will pray constantly in private and in secret.

How we might pray on Maundy Thursday

A song could be sung here.

Tomorrow (Maundy Thursday) we shall especially be living alongside Jesus' prayer in the garden of Gethsemane. According to all four Gospels, after the Last Supper Jesus left the city with his disciples for the Mount of Olives.

They appear to have stopped in an olive grove or garden in the valley, just across the River Kidron. Jesus went aside to pray: 'Abba, Father, for you all things are possible; remove this cup from me; yet, not what I want but what you want.' Evident internal strife marks this final time alone with God.

Along with the discovery of Judas' betrayal, the events of the preceding days had made it quite clear that this must be the end. Jesus had understood and affirmed God's will for him at least since the conversation with Peter at Caesarea Philippi. In the Jewish tradition in a crisis he prays that God will find a way out – trust in the providence of God – but because God is Father he prays 'Your will be done', which means 'Your kingdom come' – a difficult prayer for salvation.

So, if we are to imitate Jesus and as we know how much we are up against, but also want God's kingdom to come in us . . .

Tomorrow night provides a good way of renewing our prayer life. There may be an urgent issue, or we may be at peace. Don't be afraid, but grab the chance – bring a cushion!

How shall I pray? Consider the following:

- Knowing body, awareness, centring, slowing down, breathing.
- A slow 'Our Father'.
- Using a rosary – in lots of different ways.
- An intercessions notebook.
- Arrow prayers.
- Reading Scripture with imagination.
- Saying or reading to yourself psalms and hymns.
- Preparing for Eucharist by considering what to give thanks for, what to confess, who to pray for.
- The Jesus prayer.
- Just sitting and looking – soaking in silence. Use Psalm 46: 'Be still and know that I am God', or 'You are mine and I love you.'

- The invitation of a Desert Father to let God make you into a pillar of fire.

The worship leader may want to describe one or two of these in more detail or enable people to explore them practically.

7

Maundy Thursday

———◆•◆•◆———

The power of this night

The church lives and worships by telling and retelling the story of God among us. The clergy may well have been to the cathedral today for the renewal of their vows and to bring back to the parish the oils blessed by the bishop for the anointing of the sick and for sacraments. It may be necessary for there to be a daytime celebration but every effort should be made to bring together one congregation in the evening. Could this be several churches together and ecumenical?

Tonight we hear again and have in mind the crowded events of the Last Supper – where Jesus gave us the Eucharist and prayed for our unity in him. Invite twelve people to represent the first apostles (being sensitive about who can bear to be Judas) and a number of women to represent the women who travelled with and supported Jesus and his close disciples. As the names of the twelve are called out one by one, let them come hurriedly from all parts of the church, each carrying a stout, lighted candle. Group the candles on a table where all can see, with a larger one representing Christ. This process can be done in reverse, with reference to Jesus and the apostles going out to the garden of Gethsemane (and without the roll call) at the end of the Eucharist, before the stripping of the church. The reserved sacrament is removed from the church early in the day to enhance the sense of receiving God's gift of Eucharist in bread and wine, the gift of being united in God in all our differences, and the loving demand that we follow him in humble service. This is represented by Jesus' washing the feet of his disciples and then inviting us to 'live as I have washed your feet' – in other words, in mutual service rather than caring for people in a controlling way.

The footwashing

Chairs are arranged in a visible place for the washing of the feet and a pitcher of water, basin and towels prepared. Instead of the habitual washing of feet by an ordained minister, consider that Jesus invites us to wash one another's feet, 'as I have washed yours'. Is the minister alone representing Christ or are we all his Body? What pattern of liturgical expression best responds to Jesus' invitation in your situation? How can mutuality be expressed? Those who earlier represented the apostles (who in turn can represent all ages and all aspects of the local church's life) could be invited (with prior warning and simple rehearsal) to have their feet washed. Sitting in an arc where all can see, the 'apostles' might each have one foot washed by, say, four leaders of the church. Four towels, bowls and a single pitcher of water are all that are required. It's a practical expression of who we are as a church and so everyone should be able to watch rather than be looking at the head of the person in front or even at the page of a hymn book. Taizé chants could be the best musical solution, or two or more singers or instrumentalists, or even a CD playing in the background.

The Garden of Gethsemane

Then we keep watch with Jesus in Gethsemane until midnight, or perhaps throughout the night. This is not easy, but possibly troubling and widening our horizons. Hopefully the thought given yesterday as to how we shall pray in the silence tonight will have given us a new confidence and thirst for deepening our contact with God. Some will stay, others may return later. Tonight is our challenge to 'keep watch' for an hour in order to deepen our faith, learn to pray better or to allow God's Spirit to stir in us.

If an altar of repose for the reserved sacrament will be the focus for the vigil, it will be best honoured if the entire congregation takes part in the procession to place the reserved sacrament there. Everyone sings quietly or recites a psalm, as informally all portable decorations are removed from sight, and crosses that cannot be moved are covered to emphasize the starkness of a single cross on Good Friday.

It may be the most appropriate night of the year to encourage people to learn to pray better. The involvement of the laity can be enhanced by having more than a blanket of silence. Short prayer services led by different groups can be offered, meditating on the greatness of God's love, or on the events in Gethsemane, and so on. These should be simple, with brief readings, reflective thoughts and spontaneous prayer – to stimulate prayer in everyone. In some churches a symbolic meal of Passover food is offered at a late hour, without fuss, for people to eat simply, in church and in silence.

8

Good Friday

The way of the cross

This service of reflection for Good Friday is not intended as a substitute for the Good Friday Liturgy but may be appropriate for use with those who will not be attending the Liturgy. Again local needs may involve adapting or making use of just some of what is offered here, perhaps in combination with material from elsewhere.

A stark cross (of a size appropriate to the space) is the focus of attention.

1 The arrest

Hymn: My song is love unknown

Reading: Matthew 26.47–56

Meditation:
Notice how violence and tenderness stand together in this scene. People armed with weapons take Jesus into custody; Jesus offers no resistance, faithful to the end in carrying out the Father's mission in a way consistent with the good news. His companion, Judas, betrays him with a kiss. Although one disciple reacts with violence, Jesus heals the slave whose ear is cut off.

Try to imagine the response of the slave.

Jesus' words emphasize the vulnerable character of God's power: he could have raised resistance but refuses to do so.

Why does Jesus not ask the Father to destroy those who hand him over to mistreatment by the authorities?

His answer is strange: 'to fulfil the scriptures'. Yet Scripture is punctuated with very ordinary acts of betrayal and violence.

Anyone who is a parent or grandparent must find it hard to imagine letting anyone harm our child without reaching out in defence.

Why does the Father act in this way? Why does he choose to abandon Jesus?

How is this consistent with all that Jesus has said and done in his ministry?

Now that the disciples have escaped, Jesus is in the power of those who wish to destroy him.

Spontaneous prayer

2 Before the Sanhedrin

Hymn: Were you there when they crucified my Lord?

Reading: Matthew 26.57–68

Meditation:
The end of the story becomes clear: Jesus' death is inevitable. Jesus will remain true to his years of ministry, continuing to be obedient to his Father's will. He could say with the prophet Isaiah, 'I have set my face like flint, and I know that I shall not be put to shame; he who vindicates me is near' (Isaiah 50.7).

Provoked by his obedience, there are those who cannot bear to know God's message to the outsider and sinner.

Jesus' remark sends the High Priest into a rage and draws out sarcasm in those around.

How dare he claim to speak for God?

Recall the unnamed people in this scene. Did they wake up the next day guilt-ridden at what they had witnessed and encouraged? Was it just another day of routine sadism and brutality? Were they just obeying orders from above (as we're so familiar with hearing today)?

Where is Jesus in Iraq, Africa and Palestine, suffering unnoticed today?

'Lord, when was it that we saw you hungry or thirsty or a stranger or naked or sick or in prison, and did not take care of you?' Then he will answer them, 'Truly I tell you, just as you did not do it to one of the least of these, you did not do it to me' (Matthew 25.44f.).

Spontaneous prayer

3 Peter's denial

Hymn: Jesu grant me this I pray

Reading: Matthew 26.69–75

Meditation:

None of us would like to believe that we would behave as Peter does. In the end he surrenders to pride and self-protection, rather than admit to following Jesus. Do you ever find yourself, like me, avoiding being labelled 'Christian' by abandoning Jesus in favour of the approval of others? It's not easy to face ridicule for standing out and being different.

What I find hopeful is that Peter, even in spite of knowing he has failed, becomes a leader in the early church. If God miraculously redeems this man, there's hope that he will choose to place trust in us.

Even in spite of the times when we have left Jesus to face his agony alone, we can witness to our faith in Christ by surrendering again to his forgiveness.

Let's pray that our times of handing over faith in a positive way will eventually outnumber the times we 'hand over' Christ – not as missioners but as betrayers.

Spontaneous prayer

4 Before Pontius Pilate

Hymn: Sing my tongue

Reading: Matthew 27.11–23

Meditation:
Matthew's telling of this story is about shifting blame; he wants to show the weakness of the Roman governor and thereby place blame on the crowd – those clamouring for Jesus' death.

Let's put ourselves in the scene. If you've spoken as the crowd in the Palm Sunday liturgy you'll know what this means. We can be lulled by routine into forgetting the awful impact of what we're saying.

We are challenged to know and face the dark side in ourselves that sometimes engineers and enjoys the sufferings of others. Perhaps it's because we feel power over the situation, not feeling what others are going through.

What is your reaction to the shouting of the crowd? Do you want to react like Peter and hide? Or do you want to tell the crowd they've been tricked by their own leaders, and stand alongside Jesus?

Spontaneous prayer

5 The crowning with thorns

Hymn: The head that once was crowned

Reading: Matthew 27.27–31

Meditation:
Here is another example of those who claim to be merely acting under orders and have taken permission to act cruelly.

They may have rationalized to themselves: he deserves it.

Sometimes we aren't aware of our own cruelty: an offhand remark, a joke, a choice that makes life harder for others, the failure to take responsibility for what we say or do.

For soldiers in every age there is the temptation to enjoy baiting prisoners – it's one of the rewards of a difficult job, a way of behaving easily justified and forgotten, though in the long term corrosive of their humanity. Can you imagine being one of the soldiers?

Can you also imagine being Jesus in this situation? What are your feelings? Are you resigned, resentful, enraged, or simply numb?

What do your feelings tell you about the relationship of Jesus towards the Father, the soldiers, his disciples?

Spontaneous prayer

6 The crucifixion

Hymn: There is a green hill

Reading: Matthew 27.35–46

Meditation:
Jesus' words at the end of this text sum up his feelings. Matthew chose those words from Psalm 22.2 to describe Jesus' state just before he dies; he has deliberately chosen to complete what the Father asked of him and now experiences abandonment.

See how a willingness to be obedient to the Father has brought Jesus to this place of abandonment.

Can it be that following God's purposes can leave us feeling hopeless and alone?

Spontaneous prayer

7 Mary his mother

Hymn: Sing we of the blessed mother

Reading: John 19.25–30

Meditation:

The figure of Jesus' mother in John's text is very moving and has captured the imagination of many Christians over the centuries. Here in the story of the crucifixion, we see the completion of what the prophet Simeon said when Mary and Joseph brought Jesus to the temple: 'This child is destined for the falling and the rising of many in Israel, and to be a sign that will be opposed so that the inner thoughts of many will be revealed – and a sword will pierce your own soul too' (Luke 2.34f.). The sacred poem *Stabat mater*, attributed to the thirteenth-century Franciscan Jacapone da Todi, tells of her pain.

> The mother of sorrows stood in tears beside the cross on which her son was hanging.
> Her grieving heart, anguished and lamenting, was pierced by a sword;
> How sad and afflicted was that Blessed Mother for her only Son,
> For she grieved and sorrowed, the pious Mother, as she witnessed the pains of her great Son.
> Where is the one who would not weep to see the Mother of Christ in such suffering?

Who would not share her sorrow, seeing the loving Mother grieving with her Son?

For the sins of his people, she saw Jesus in torment and subdued with whips.

She saw her dear son dying, forsaken, as he yielded up his Spirit.

Mother of Jesus, make me to feel the strength of your grief, so that I may mourn with you!

Make my heart burn with love for Christ, my Lord God, that I may be pleasing to him!

Holy Mother, this I pray, drive the wound of the Crucified deep into my heart.

Share with me the pains of your wounded Son who is so gracious to suffer for my sake.

Make me truly weep with you, and share the suffering of the crucified, as long as I shall live.

To stand with you beside the cross, and share your grief is my desire.

Let me bear the death of Christ, be a sharer of his passion, contemplate his wounds!

Let me suffer his pain, let me be engulfed by the cross, for the love of your son.

Grant that I may be defended by the cross, learn its message of self-giving love, be strengthened by Christ's grace.

When my body dies, may I know the glory of paradise. Amen.

(slightly amended)

9

Holy Saturday

———◆•◆———

Holy Saturday usually has little impact in comparison with Good Friday. It gets merged into Easter Day or lost in flower-arranging and furniture-moving. Holy Saturday symbolizes Christ's sojourn in the tomb but our liturgies have offered little to mark this important second day. It's uncomfortable and so we have preferred to avoid it. But there are moves throughout the church today to discover the promise of reflection on what it means for us that Christ descended to the dead. It takes courage not to hide the awkwardness and fear of a church in exile, knowing lostness and stubbornly refusing to die. It's really difficult to accept that we are witnessing the unravelling of the world as it was. They really don't work any more – the old securities of power and the reservoirs of heritage, learning, reliable empires and trusted certitudes. Some even try to recruit the church to support the yearning in society that imagines the old certainties will continue to serve.

The letter to Galatians (5.22) invites us to live with patience through days of uncertainty, not knowing and brokenness. Holy Saturday is a day to read Scripture, to expect and look for spiritual restoration and renewal, to create intimate and attractive community, to preach and teach and devise liturgy intentionally to imagine and practise a new obedience to God's mission. How shall we weave God's future church? Only by listening and speaking to God and learning who God is. Then we are in a position to practise and invite discipleship that values tolerance, mutual love and compromise.

Such conversation implies an initial silence. Before there can be sound or speech there has to be silence. Just before a concert or a speech there is a brief call for silence. Our worship only has impact on us when it's deliberately seen as speech rooted in silence. It's as if there can only be black letters printed if there is a white page against which to contrast them. The words we speak – in church or in any situation – are so import-ant that they need to come out of silence. In church, politics, education or family we lose out when we don't punctuate life deliberately with silence or reflection.

The Scriptures show us God waiting with us in desert places, inviting the patience of 40 days and 40 nights. This waiting – for Elijah, John the Baptist and Jesus – provides a tap root into the self-energizing life and newness of God. God time and time again – in the face of the amazing darkness of human activity such as the death camps of world conflicts – reveals a capacity to arise and devour the powers of death. In the darkened church on Holy Saturday the faithful await the God who stirs, who forms light and creates darkness, who bestows blessing and creates woe. This is the Lord who does all these things. Our God is self-starting, always re-energizing, brings grief to glory, discovers newness, transforms death to life, breaks the powers of the night, displays a fresh mobilization of the resolve spoken to our ancestors.

Many of us lack courage for truth telling. Holy Saturday gives us new heart from our ancestors in the faith who opposed the dominant myths of slavery, market forces, gender prejudice and countless injustices – in the energy of the God who defeats the powers. And let's not overlook that in our world the church is called out on so many occasions to prove that death is not the final word – funerals, tragedies, illnesses, breakdowns, departed glory. Part of our calling as ministers of the church is to have conversed with God long enough to have the capacity to listen and maybe to have something to say that has integrity because we have dared to listen to the experience of those living in the hell of in-between-spaces.

A liturgy for Holy Saturday

I believe, from experience in planning and using it with a parish group, that in *Holy Saturday Faith* Ian Wallis has provided a fertile beginning for considering a liturgy that encapsulates these themes (see pages 162–172). An altar represents the tomb where Jesus is laid. Beginning with the refusal to give up on hope in the God who saves (Habakkuk 3.17–18), Wallis sets the scene with John's account of the burial of Jesus (John 19.38–42). Then with verses from the book of Job, we pray a Jewish prayer of mourning: 'I sit and gnaw on my grief; my groans pour out like water' (Job 3.24, quoted in Wallis page 163).

Then, while worshippers mark themselves with ash, songs of sorrow and lament (e.g. Psalms 137 and 88) can be said or sung: 'Will your wonders be known in the dark? or your right-eousness in the country where all is forgotten?' (Psalm 88.12, *Celebrating Common Prayer*, page 600.).

Attention is then given to the Scriptures in Chapter 53 of the prophet Isaiah's revelation of God's redeeming hand. In response, as a devotion come verses from the Song of Songs: 'love is as strong as death' (8.6–7).

A candle is lit and placed at the foot of the altar while a short prayer and words of comfort are read (Psalms 23 and 139). The first chapter of the book of Ruth gives testimony to recogniz-ing God's love and human faithfulness even in death. During the singing of the hymn and recitation of the psalm, worshippers are invited to light a candle and to place it at the foot of the altar, representing the tomb where Jesus was laid.

Then follows a series of biddings, a mixture of structure and spontaneity, remembering Jesus by the lakeside, his stories and sayings, when he touched lepers, when he taught us to pray, and eventually to 'I remember when they came to arrest him . . . [and] when they strung him up on a cross to die.' This culminates in praying as Jesus taught us.

The liturgy comes to a close in embracing the legacy of Jesus: 'Through the telling of the stories, the study of the Scriptures, the following of the way, the breaking of the bread, the practice of forgiveness', and so on, concluding with a Blessing of God's Holy Name in the Mourner's Kaddish Prayer.

Variations on this outline, with hymns and silences, will bear a great deal of trial and error. I have found that a short address flows naturally from the key components of the legacy of Jesus identified by Wallis (in chapter 6). The legacy of Jesus that we embrace through tears on this day will inspire us to continue being a community rooted in six deep principles:

1 *Embodying forgiveness.* Jesus shows and brings us God's own generosity, from which arises the invitation for us to be human in that way, demonstrating a disturbing quality of forgiveness and overflowing inclusion, at whatever cost.
2 *Living (the) prayer.* Orientated by the Lord's Prayer, we desire to become a community that shows what it is like when God's kingdom draws near. Drawn into the Trinity, instinctively, we follow the inspiration of Jesus, the way of God's children. We allow Jesus' own prayerfulness to fill our lives and that of our community.
3 *Purveying wisdom.* We believe that theology is the work and privilege of all. The Bible is an open book for all; the community makes space for all to explore the meaning

of faith and life together. Wisdom is not the preserve of the merely clever. Prayer thinking is the shared responsibility of all as we give from our different experiences and ways of knowing.

4 *Living generously.* Jesus' meals, God's blessings and hospitality are a pattern for our community. Costly sacrifice involves mutuality not domination; being last, offering even our shirt, and learning to be footwashers are key. The words and actions of the Last Supper shape our living. We become constantly thankful, eucharistic, filled with praise through God's gift to us. So we learn to practise community and faithfully perform the gospel for the world's sake.

5 *Nurturing love.* Jesus was formed both by his family and local synagogue. He demonstrated and taught mutual obligation, the forming of persons who show God's love, relationships of justice, integrity and trust, that are costly to self. His own relationship with the Father makes possible the living by communities of the new commandment 'that you love one another as I have loved you'. This means the learning of how to delight in one another's good and growing church as a sign of the potential of all relationships, personal and global.

6 *Keeping faith.* To embrace the legacy of Jesus will mean keeping faith alive together. Baptism is the key to becoming cross-shaped like Jesus, and pursuing the way of holiness, filled with God's life. The church exists to give others access to the faith of Jesus. This requires church to be a reading of the good news, an open book of the gospel. We are called to recognize the presence of Jesus in daily life and to see our everyday places as a way of the cross in which Christ, as companion, is present.

10

Easter Day

The vigil

Let's look ahead now to our keeping of the Easter Vigil early on Sunday morning. The central drama of our faith and the world's history is enacted over three days from Good Friday (the cross), through Holy Saturday (burial) to the Day of Resurrection. We observed Good Friday at one of the services available. This will have had the feel of the devastation and grief of those who thought this dreadful death was the end of all their hope. Holy Saturday is the day of emptiness, the day after the end, the day of mourning and of sharing important memories of Jesus who is now in the tomb. Then, unexpectedly, with the vigil early on Sunday morning comes God's self-starting, renewed, glorious Easter life.

To grasp the central idea of the Easter Vigil we need to link it to the Jewish experience of freedom from slavery. The Jews, from the time of their original exodus from Egypt, would spend this entire night in watching and prayer, dressed in garments for travelling, with staves in their hands.

The first reason for it was to celebrate their liberation in the past, to bring back vividly to their minds the most important event in their history, their becoming the chosen people of God. There was another, even more important reason and purpose. Something at the vigil was very alive.

More than remembering the past they were earnestly looking to the future, expecting God to act in a new way.

While recalling that God had 'passed among' his people in days gone by, they were consciously waiting for God to pass among his people yet again. They were waiting for 'him who was to come' – their long-promised Messiah. Their liberation in days gone by pointed to a new liberation which, they knew, might come at any time.

The Jewish religion is very forward-looking, full of expectancy. The Christian church looks back as well as forward. We remember a day of deliverance on the cross when Christ made us God's people too. But we also look forward as we cannot ignore the fact that we know what the first disciples could not. We are waiting for the risen Lord to come among his people again, with open hearts and minds. So the vigil is not a bit of historical archaeology about what early Christians used to do. It's an active climax to the events of Holy Week closely linked with the history of God among the Jews, the first Christians experiencing Christ's risen presence, Pentecost and then 2,000 years of Christian experience across the world in every country.

We start the vigil with the lighting of a fire (as large and lively as is safe) to symbolize the heat and energy of God's resurrection life filling Christ as he rises from the tomb. It is the fire of God's irrepressible love offered to our hearts, a love that never runs out.

We take a very large candle on which is inscribed Alpha and Omega – the first and last letters of the Greek alphabet. The liturgy helps us dramatically to proclaim that Christ is the beginning and the end: the beginning of our salvation when he came among us as Jesus of Nazareth, and the end of it when he will come at the end of time. Easter is a reminder and a promise of both.

The candle is also marked with the five wounds of Christ, so representing Christ himself. It is then lit and becomes even more Christ-like – for Christ brought life in all its fullness; he is the Light of the World. 'Christ our light', sings the deacon. 'Thanks be to God', we reply, greeting the light that shines in the darkness of our hearts and of the world.

We enter the church, led by the candle symbolizing the pillar of fire, as the Israelites were led by the pillar of fire on the night of their liberation. Christ is our light and in him we become light, as the first apostles and disciples were flooded with a new life. But in our turn we have the task of filling our families, community and wherever we go with this same light of Christ as a celebration of our salvation.

Next, one (or two, as a duet) sings the paschal proclamation, proclaiming to us the glory of this night in a song known as the 'Exultet'. We are invited to rejoice in the triumph of the mighty king who has risen and conquered death and sin.

> This is our Passover feast
> when Christ the true lamb is slain
> – the night when you freed the people of Israel from their slavery
> – when Christians everywhere
> washed clean of sin
> and freed of all defilement
> are restored to grace and grow together in holiness.
>
> This is the night when Jesus Christ
> broke the chains of death
> and rose triumphant from the grave.

Then we listen to Scripture readings, the story of our redemption. We may not have all the readings telling about the original creation that foreshadowed the new creation that Christ has effected in us; we are told of Isaac, the beloved son, designated for a sacrificial death, and of God's promise to Abraham; then we are reminded of the Passover of the Jews and of prophecies concerning the Saviour who was still to come in order to make us into a chosen Christian people, to be led by him into the new promised land.

But the Jews were constituted into a people only by passing through the waters of the Red Sea. Our constitution as a people took place in a similar manner, as we all passed through the waters of baptism. In the words of Paul we are instructed about the meaning of baptism: 'When we were baptized we went into the tomb with Christ and joined him in death, so that as he was raised from the dead by the father's glory, we too might live a new life.' We then sing 'Alleluia' and listen to the Gospel account of the empty tomb. Christ is indeed risen!

Celebrating the resurrection of Christ, we celebrate also the resurrection of all humanity and creation of which baptism is the sacrament. The wonder of our baptism is among the chief lessons we have to learn that night. So we pray with all who in the past have been through the waters of baptism – the saints of every age.

We then bless the baptismal water with words that remind us of the many wonders God has done when the people of Israel faced a situation that seemed to have no resolution; near the end of this prayer the priest takes the Easter candle that represents Christ, and plunges it into the water to remind us of the descent of Christ into his grave:

> May all who are buried with Christ
> in the death of baptism
> rise also with him to newness of life.

And when the candle is lifted from the water as Christ was raised from the tomb we greet this symbol of resurrection with a joyful response. Candidates for baptism are baptized at this point, and there will be a renewal of vows for all of us.

Then we follow Christ's command and take bread and wine in his name. On that night he will come; the Lord will pass over each one of us and over us as a community. He will actually come into our hearts as we all share this experience and share the sacraments together.

But it will be more than a memory of the past; more even than the making a present of the past. It will also be the pledge of astonishing future glory. For we shall be eating of the bread of which if we eat we shall live for ever: 'If anyone eats my flesh', says the lord and master, 'I shall raise him up on the last day.'

And so our Easter vigil and communion will be a fitting conclusion to this week, a foretaste of the love and laughter of heaven.

11

Easter reflection 1

The weeks of Easter are there to help us pray and think again how to be a church shaped by the cross and resurrection. The first disciples were puzzled and anxious, as well as filled with joy and new hope. We, like them, are offered a new beginning, a time for reflecting on how to become more the church God needs in society and the world now. Archbishop Michael Ramsey spoke of Easter as the fault line in history. When God raised Jesus Christ from the tomb nothing would ever be the same again. Imagine going on the beach in the dark with a torch. You walk to the water's edge and shine your torch on the sea. To say that you understand resurrection is to be looking at a tiny pool of light and claiming to know the entire ocean.

Prayer

Reading: John 20.19–31

> As storytellers
> we shape your
> unfolding story
>
> as passionate people
> we share your
> passion for justice

as bearers of God
we embody your life
in the world

HUMBLE US TO LISTEN
TO FORGOTTEN STORIES

EMPOWER US WITH BOLDNESS
WHEN WE ARE AFRAID

RE-SOURCE US
FOR THE BIRTHING OF LIBERATION
(Ruth Burgess and Chris Polhill, *Eggs and Ashes*, p. 226)

Daring to let God Easter us

Understanding the mystery of the resurrection with our minds
is ambitious. Down the centuries Christians have tried many
different ways of expressing Easter faith – and discovered that
we need a cluster of varied pictures, held together. It's about
new birth, new creation, new hope, acceptance by God, a fresh
start in forgiveness, a new community across all barriers, a
filling up by the Holy Spirit, the presence in our lives of the
risen Jesus Christ . . . and that's only a beginning.

Let's start rather with our need for the risen Christ. Our
own hearts and the newspapers provide us with a catalogue
of problems, stresses, sources of anger and general fearfulness
that threaten to overwhelm us. At Easter we stand with the
astonished first disciples, faced with an empty tomb and confused by several encounters with the patient and forgiving
risen Jesus. Jesus was preparing them, in the momentous days
after Easter, for their own task. Now they were to be filled with
the Spirit as a transformed, believing community. They were
to share in the same mission from God in which Jesus had

died and to which they had been called. They were able to say, 'Jesus is Lord – God raised him from the dead.'

This is true for us now. Do we dare to perceive the over-flowing blessings we are being given and to what awesome responsibility we are summoned? When Comic Relief was on the television recently I was struck by the explosive good will, generosity and humour of thousands of people. The marches at the time of the G8 Summit had a similar impact. Working to eradicate poverty in Africa as a matter of justice had caught the imagination of a large part of the Western world. Apart from the speeches by church leaders, there was no explicit reference to faith. I was reminded of the missionary commitment of our churches in the nineteenth and early twentieth centuries. It was a reversal. Now it was secular good will, passionate for repairing the world and its people, while religious people often seem more concerned with policing one another's personal behaviour or deciding who can do what in church leadership.

The risen Christ in every age reaches out to us. He brings joy and hope to our individual lives, if we can receive forgive-ness, reassurance and discipline. We can be transformed by surrendering and allowing God's love to fill our darkest places. We need to put up a white flag and admit we cannot, try as we may, make sense of our lives on our own. The ministry of Jesus gave us many examples of the meaning of 'entering into the master's joy', invited to the feast of the kingdom, the last coming first. We cannot be bystanders, looking on and saying, 'How interesting'. We either reject God's offer in Jesus or we dare to risk being overtaken by it. As Nicodemus found, private warm support for Jesus' cause is not an option. Just as God gives without reservation – like all the new good-quality wine at Cana – so we are called to respond with all of ourselves. Resur-rection cannot be made to fit our world-view – rather we are invited to be part of a resurrection world-view.

> In a small group or alone, ask what this risky overtaking could mean for yourself or for your church now.

This story illustrates the trust Jesus invites. Long ago a king invited his wealthy courtiers to come to celebrate his birthday at the royal palace. The king made it clear that he expected a present. He boldly asked each one to bring a bowl, goblet or box made out of gold. Some were generous and brought large gold cups – maybe they wanted to show off their own wealth – while others were cautious and mean and with a grumble brought just a small gold box. The king had laid on a great feast with music and dancing. Halfway through the proceedings he clapped his hands for silence. 'And now we come to the high spot of the evening,' he said. 'Please come forward with your presents for my birthday.' So one by one they came and offered their gifts – the containers made of gold, some huge and some tiny. Imagine their surprise, however, when as each one handed over the gift, it was immediately taken by the king's steward and filled with diamonds. 'Thank you,' said the king. 'My real intention was to give *you* a gift.' And he handed back the gold containers, holding as many diamonds as there was room for!

So we are invited to be filled with the gifts of the Spirit in all the places in which we have made room for the risen Christ.

> Alone or in twos, consider what gift of the Spirit you have been given and how to let it work more fully for the good of others.

And Jesus also invites us to be a community, a community of commitment. The church of God does not have a mission –

but the God of mission has a church, and that's you and me, expanded by Easter joy. Like the very first witnesses, filled with the Spirit, we are changed by the presence of Christ – his Spirit is with us. We are not called to test the truth of the resurrection, but to let it test us. We have been born anew to a living hope, shaped by the worship of God.

How is God calling my church to take part in the mission that Jesus began when he came saying, 'The kingdom of God has come close'?

Following Jesus could mean a practice of singing, contemplation, hospitality, entertaining without expectation, forgiveness of wrongs, actively seeking reconciliation with those from whom we are estranged, courtesy, respect, seeking to put right injustices, inclusiveness, to see glory in the face of all others. This is the scandal that brought Jesus to the cross. If we were convicted of being an Easter people, would the evidence hold up in court? Are we truly subversive in opposing all that enslaves, oppresses or denies the dignity of others or the created world?

I believe that Western society has an urgent need for churches that deliberately practise the gospel so confidently and openly that others can understand and respond with their whole being. The purpose of this book is to stimulate Christian groups to think, interact and pray together as they continue to ask the Holy Spirit to help discern their own calling by God. As a result they will grow in their capacity to serve society and to show the world the effects of placing trust in Christ's love.

As God is present in every place and moment, there is no point in churches being anxious about their survival or even growth. God certainly has no need of our protection. Two thousand years of experiment in how to be church reveals many contrasting forms that have been and gone; the future has many more in store. The task of each local church is to be the visible practice of Christian faith, deliberately to become a true performance of the good news.

Christian speech and action for the world's repairing flows from the experience of being deeply loved by God the Holy Trinity. The open love of God comes to us through praise, prayer, Scripture reading, sacraments and imagining, thinking and questioning together. The encouragement of every member of a congregation to spend regular time in a small group or cell meeting is a priority today for the church to grow in its identity, intimacy and confidence.

One of the key tasks for the Christian community now is to show the world its true potential. By our enactment of the gospel – in words, relationships, attitudes, caring and reaching out – we offer a glimpse of God's final hope for the world. The life of the world, of neighbourhoods and of people together is hard to navigate. As a gospel people we have to search and argue together, to find good shapes and rhythms for living. Mission Action Planning is the way in which our Easter joy is being channelled in many churches at present.

The letters of Paul to excited and struggling new Christian communities offer both encouragement and warning. If we risk leaving behind safe, comfortable, non-threatening ways of being church and choose more intimacy with God and one another, we need to watch out! We need to check triangles of complaint, patterns of blame, false extreme alternative positions and the ways of projecting our fears on to others. Moving deliberately from infantilizing hierarchical patterns to ways of mutual responsibility draws out our need for growing in patience with ourselves and others, calling on ever deeper wells of Scripture, silence and prayer, and being formed as eucharistic people – above all knowing how much God has blessed us already and how much more God wants us to have, to know and to become.

> Discuss (or consider for yourself) one or two practical steps for yourself and your church.

The future of our church is as an embodiment of good news. Instead of fearing difference, which is the way of the world, our worship of the Holy Trinity opens us joyfully to rejoicing in difference. We need to take up our equal responsibilities through differing skills and imaginations, to engage in this challenge. Together we can be catholic, evangelical, protestant, orthodox, traditional and radical – all things to all people, engaging in all of life. What is not allowed is watching from the side to see what happens. Our society needs a church that is prepared to struggle in the midst of issues of identity, race, gender, poverty, education, prisons and so on, neither being accommodated to the culture entirely nor pulling up the draw-bridge of purity. Secure in our role, we can work on the edge and at the centre of society as needed.

But we shall not find our role simply by working for the revival of the church's fortunes. Revivalism, or working harder to recreate the past, is not part of the church's way. Although we are inheritors of many great traditions – of speech, singing, patterns of authority, ways of worshipping, understanding God's ways – and although we can be grateful for the past, there is no excuse for not doing our work now in our own generation. I sometimes think of church history as a long knitted scarf, still on the needles. You can admire the many different colours and patterns that have brought us to here, but the imagination must move us on. The church is not like a ship, buffeted through the waves, but essentially and reliably the same. The practical expression of Christian faith – church – has to be found again and again in every new moment and place. With young people and all to whom we reach out we must have the courage to be spontaneous and truthful. The temptation is to try to draw them to where we are or where we think they ought to be. The real test is, do we have the courage to go with them to a new place, where neither we nor they have ever been before?

The mainline churches have no guaranteed future. In 2,000 years, many forms of church have come and gone. Resurrection life gives us the power to be vulnerable, to live without security, to discover again who we need to be as a church in this place at this time. The only success we need is to be a faithful expression of the church, responding to God at work in the world. Size may not be crucial.

What is vital is attending to discipleship. In our different ways of following the risen Christ we all need support – spiritual companionship, a rule of life, worship that feeds us. It means recovering a knowledge of biblical speech, a language for making Christian meaning in the world, inhabiting the unfolding story of God with us, that Jesus demonstrated so intensely.

It will mean discerning what forms of ministry we need to grow in order to serve the needs and develop the hope of many people and neighbourhoods, beyond what is familiar. It will mean reassessing the effectiveness of our witness in all the places we work, live and help local networks to flourish. Are we supporting ourselves as the church so dispersed? If ministry is to be interactive, collaborative and mutual, what is the particular role of the priest and lay ministers? Are we giving them space to be animators and leaders by taking our full share of responsibility for making church happen?

In short, the church of the risen Christ today is called to recover the adventure of being a holy church in the ordinary details of life – locally and globally. We need both ideas and bodies to make it work. Ideas, because words are given to us by God to imagine what we might be. Bodies, because the whole of Christ is risen from the dead. So, the Spirit calls us to be a community of distinctive character, in which everyone enacts the performance of the life of Jesus who is our Lord.

12

Easter reflection 2

Prayer

Read John 17.1–19 – Christ builds us into a new community to be sent into the world.

> O God, you Easter our hearts.
> Help us now to see how to take up the fullest possibility of
> our lives,
> to grow in love together
> so that our hearts are on fire
> as an inspiration and an alluring call to all those around us
> to share in your living presence.

Revisit the exercise in self-awareness (pages 17 and 25).

Re-membered by the Eucharist

The eucharistic celebration is a sign of God's deep love for the world until Christ comes in glory. Through our participation over time we are absorbed into Christ's life, death and resurrection. In eucharistic living over time we are taken apart and reconstituted by God's probing love. Each element has its own importance and in none of them are we merely passive.

We greet one another in Christ's name.
It's a choice merely to be reticent or talk to those we know well; to make Eucharist as a full participant we need to be open and generous to others as well as respecting their space.

We share the Scriptures.
If we know what the readings are to be in church beforehand, which is not difficult to arrange, we can have read and reflected on them before their public reading and before the sermon. This is one way to be interactive. In some churches occasionally a group plan a sermon together for the preacher to preach. There are many ways we could imagine of sharing the breaking of the Word.

We share a concern for the needs of the church and the world.
What about experimenting with the intercessions – a small group planning them together, more silence or spontaneity, or inviting one or two people to be ready to speak briefly about their work or life experience or concern for the world and turn it into prayer? Overstretched clergy probably need someone else to set this in motion and keep an eye on its development.

We share the peace in all our difference.
The sharing of the peace can become a routine of handshaking with all kinds of power games being unconsciously played out. It calls for our growing sense of awareness. Imagine it as yet another commitment to enjoy the amazing difference between us. Use it as an incremental covenant to work for the repair of the world in each place in which someone here has influence. Together, again, we commit ourselves to the project of God that Jesus calls the coming reign or kingdom.

We share bread and wine.
Think of ways of deepening this dimension, perhaps through larger, more generous and earthy portions of bread and wine.

I have experienced the bread once broken being distributed to everyone to hold carefully until everyone has their share, before all respond to the invitation to receive with a corporate Amen, consuming the bread in unison.

We share a common life.
Are we pretending to be a community, or maybe not even pretending? Many of us are introverted by inclination and have to work at close contact. Taking care of one another as well as asking more from one another is part of discipleship. How we allow for a wide variety of expressions of worship and life together is a test of our understanding that we are many parts of Christ's body. None of us should expect church to be indulgent to our literary or musical tastes but we could expect to have some of what we find helpful and awesome once in a while.

We share a common ministry.
Christ is the fount of all ministry. The church is that group of people who have accepted God's forgiveness and the grace and call to repair the world. Despite years of new language about mission, discipleship, evangelism and the ministry of all, we choose on the whole to be Christians to varying degrees. The more the laity see themselves as the church God needs for the sake of the world and to be formed for that task, the more those who are ordained have a demanding and unique role to play. When shall we be able to move beyond the old polarity of one or the other? Our trinitarian God who is a *koinonia* of difference in relation invites us to recognize the many-faceted and never static nature of the ministry in which we have an equal share.

We discern God's truth for the world.
The church community, steeped in its chief asset, Christian faith itself, recognizes the contribution of everyone. Some

know well the church's Scriptures and tradition of belief; others know God through music and song; others know God in the newspapers and current debate; others work with God in politics and social service; others are rooted in God through prayer; others in serving the young; some know God in academic knowledge, education and the money markets. Whether in worship or at work or in the family, we are called to show the world its true life. To do this we need to be growing in awareness ourselves of how our everyday tracks are filled with and critiqued by the patterns of God shown to us through the Spirit in the life, death and resurrection of Jesus Christ.

We become a sign of a new way of being human.
The bottom line is that God is probably less interested in religion than are we. The Eucharist enables us to practise the kind of *koinonia* community that questions every assumption and turns the world upside down. Our church's problems are not important. We are not called to cosiness and piety. Our living and dying is to be formed as workers with God for the world's repairing.

Small group or personal work: Our daily blessings

As we consider this list, can we recognize God at work in our lives, inviting us to give and not to count the cost? We may not have all of these but it's unlikely we don't have most of them:

- Food for our body
- Stimulation for our mind
- Music, sounds
- Friends

- Church community life
- Associations and organizations that claim our attention

- What or who are you thankful for at this moment?
- What are the principles (choose three) by which you live – that you would die for? e.g. fairness, justice, peace, standing up for those on the edge.
- Give thanks for your many blessings – in what ways could you increase your generosity or live with more risk for others?
- So are we half-full or half-empty?

Let each person take a moment to consider and write on a Post-it note one person or thing for which you are thankful at this moment. Then let everyone stick their Post-it note (anonymously) on a large sheet of paper or somewhere central so all can see.

The leader might highlight some of these. Some group members may want to add their own voices.

Closing worship

A form of night prayer might be used, perhaps from the Iona Community (Wild Goose Publications) or *A New Zealand Prayer Book*, including some scripture passages.

13

Expecting the Holy Spirit

Prayer

Reading: Matthew 3.13—4.20

Referring back to the exercise in self-awareness (pages 17 and 25), spend a time in silence alone or in the group.

Using the following outline if helpful, pray together spontaneously for the renewed presence of the Holy Spirit to your heart and mind, your church and local community.

Lord, send your Spirit upon us,
the Spirit you promised,
that we may choose to live fully
as your chosen people,
as you have come near as our faithful God.

Help us to grow in faith and love
with and through the leaders of our church
and all your people
in every place and time.

Draw us together,
with the strength
that is the particular quality of your loving kindness.
So that, wherever we are,
together and alone,

we become more and more the sign
of your active, loving presence
in every single part of our world.

In all our glorious difference,
unite us in the energy known to us as the Holy Spirit.

Becoming a community of hope

All our striving for success and control is so much pride and grandiosity. The real journey begins when we allow that our starting point is knowing that God takes the initiative. Before we turn to God, we are already regarded and beloved. The practice of Christian community provides a home where we are invited to know that we are deeply loved temples of the Holy Spirit. We make a start by giving up having to make life work well through our own effort. Like the returning prodigal, our only way is to receive the embrace and luxurious welcome of the Father. Then we are released to risk losing life to find it in following Christ. At the heart of the gospel there is nothing but God's initiative of love, which is infinite, sacrificial and life-giving, respecting our freedom 'to death, even death on a cross' (Philippians 2.8).

The world needs churches that set out to respond to God's loving kindness by deliberately becoming welcoming but tough communities of the new order of love. The hope that Christians bring to society lies precisely in being formed, through a lifetime's love affair with God. So we are free to be formed and called to show and tell the truth about living. In all the mess of the world, churches live the baptized way of life, called and infused by Christian faith, in which we are shaped in our own identity and anticipate how God will one day remake all things.

Making God's truth visible is the faithful corporate performance of what churches know of God's speech and ways of acting in the life of Israel and of Jesus. The interaction of the persons of the Trinity towards each other and towards all created being is an active demonstration of who God is.

In theatre, ballet, dance, poetry reading and musical expression, there is no higher calling than to performance that is freighted with the values and love of writer, actor and audience. Understanding with body, mind and spirit is demonstrated in rehearsed, strenuous, risky and demanding public practice. The saying, writing, preparation and presentation are all equally parts of the performance or drama. Similarly within the discipline we call church there will be suffering as well as joy, intensity as well as relaxed enjoyment, thinking and worshipping, telling out and demonstrating.

Small group or individual work

If you are to become part of a community of the love of Jesus, what steps or attitudes will be needed?

For example, recall how the first disciples (150 of them) prayed together in the upper room. Read Acts 1.11–15 and 2.1–4. How shall we take time for withdrawal from the pressures of the world, to relearn and experience how deeply we are loved and what God now expects of us?

Or consider how through knowing such divine acceptance, each of us can bear to face the extent to which our human nature has been damaged. Rather than pushing blame and projections on to others, love enables the self to bear the pain of its own disunity and hostility.

Again, dissatisfaction or restlessness of the heart, self-criticism, and yearning for fulfilment are important elements of discipleship provided that first we know that nothing can separate us from God's overflowing love. What do we want to see changed in our church and ourselves? How can we become agents of that change?

Instead of mere tolerance of the other, Christian community rejoices to include, celebrate and work with many in dialogue, closeness and trust. How could we be deliberately more inclusive of difference? Where would we begin? With enquirers or occasional visitors? Or with ethical choices, a new awareness of human rights and justice for all?

Acting in good faith

The world needs Christian communities of those who know what it is to be free, those on the way to becoming authentic. The easier option is to live in imitation of others or to stop speaking or acting honestly for fear of giving offence. Jesus invites his followers to recast our human behaviour by checking the temptation to accommodate ourselves to outside opinion. Instead we are invited to speak from the self that is loved by and has put on Christ.

When we catch on to this, acting from within, freedom will become a quality, an experience of self, a state of mind, like joy and peace; and this is the freedom that (truly self-) controls. How many free people do you know? They are worth following.

Knowing that we are the beloved of God makes it possible to set out on a tough journey that takes us to a level of awareness some have called the 'true' or 'essential' self or the 'real' I. As we have seen earlier, learning to monitor our lives and to check

111

the impact of all kinds we have on others day by day, is to access the human gift of 'self-reflective consciousness', deeper than normal awareness. The twentieth-century spiritual pioneer Thomas Merton describes the potential in everyone to know the 'diamond' blazing as a point of pure truth, 'the gate of heaven' in each one of us. Christian community living is an invitation to break through, step by step, into a greater sense of our authentic or real authority as Christians and as leaders. It is no easy matter.

The performance of Christian community includes learning wisdom in how we react both to criticism and praise in relating. To experience deep acceptance releases us from being too fragile to receive criticism or rejection. When we live from our false self we cannot bear to be wrong and easily rush into denial, defence and self-pity. Equally, we move beyond needing to be proved right or to know our worth only in terms of approved behaviour, acknowledged achievements, possessions, appreciation or popular approval.

We open ourselves to God in prayer so that our true self may blossom. We look to the transformation of the self through trusting openness to the presence of the Holy Trinity. Our journey of bodily and mindful awareness is about becoming less self-centred, less touchy and prickly, less gullible and fearful.

Steeped in the patterns of prayer, Eucharist, worship, Bible study, imaginative reflection and silence, dying to our fearful, vain and self-important self, we find an inner centre and a grounded self, the authentic self-understanding of the Christlike love that casts out fear (1 John 4.18). Regular participation in the Eucharist, centring on the cross, makes its deepening mark on us, as gradually, sometimes dramatically, we come to live the real life to which God invites us, attracted by a goodness and beauty that makes all things possible.

Growing up together

Reading: Ephesians 3.16–19

Christian contemplation or meditation, being totally open to God, is not a private, narcissistic programme for self-development. Rather, transformative church communities, constituted by Christians growing up together as learning to be true disciples, offer to society the practice of living with ambiguity. Christians know they are neither angels nor demons. In each one exists both a divine spark and a powerful leaning towards evil. Jesus recognized just how intertwined are these forces when he announced that you cannot pull out weeds without damaging healthy plants (Matthew 13.24–30, 36–43).

The dividing line between good and evil cuts through the heart of every human being. Leaving behind the compulsive fear and pressure of the attitude (so powerfully reinforced by the press) that we are either a total success or a desperate failure is one of the graces given through opening up ourselves to the freedom of the Holy Spirit.

One of the greatest contributions of the performance of Christian community to society is the potential for awakening inner awareness as our relationship with God deepens and grows. Such discipline gives a growing personal power, in each decision, to move from a preoccupation with ourselves to acting with love for God, so providing a passover, or bridge from the false self to the authentic person we are called to be. Mystics such as St John of the Cross push us to stop wrestling with our shame and difficulties and be taken over in a love affair with God. To fall in love and stay in love with God will decide every part of life.

Learning to live with contradictions and paradoxes is an essential work of the church for itself and the world. It's about loving our enemies, respecting our wounds, and celebrating the very things that make us stumble, slow us down, and frustrate and frighten us. Rather than simply move on from difficulties, we need to travel with and through dark memories, to reach healing and growth.

Prayers in expectation of the coming of the Holy Spirit

Beginning with the leader, focusing on a candle or some other symbol in the middle of the group, or holding a stone passed from one to another, pray using the simple formula:

'I pray for a church that . . .'

The leader needs to hold the expectant silence for longer than may be natural, to allow for less confident voices to come to the surface. When all who wish to speak have done so, conclude with the following or some other prayer:

Welcoming the future – turbulent and deeply satisfying

We ask you, Holy Spirit, to blow your wind on us,
to knock us sideways,
to warm our hearts,
to transpose us to a new key.
Shake us out of the attitude that we haven't enough,
and show us the overwhelming superabundance of your life among us.
Give us the imagination to see the abundance of all you give us,
to recognize your blessings in Jesus Christ
and to become agents of God's work in the world.

Our trust lies in the One who has called us.
May our living Lord bless us and our community
to be a sign of hope to all people,
Father, Son, and Holy Spirit.
Amen.

As a mutual blessing, invite worshippers to learn the simple prayer 'May God the Holy Spirit bless you deeply' by repeating it two or three times. Then, rather like sharing the peace, invite everyone to weave among the group, encouraging touching as people choose, saying the blessing prayer to one another. As this might take a few minutes, music could be played while people pray with each other, then continue by sharing simple food and drink before leaving.

Resources and further reading

Au, Wilkie, SJ, 1992, *By Way of the Heart: Towards a Holistic Spirituality*, London, Geoffrey Chapman.

Bell, John L., 2003, *Wrestle and Fight and Pray: Christianity and Conflict*, Edinburgh, St Andrew Press.

Bourgeault, Cynthia, 2004, *Centering Prayer and Inner Awakening*, Cambridge, MA, Cowley Publications.

Brueggemann, Walter, 2003, *Awed to Heaven, Rooted in Earth*, Minneapolis, MN, Fortress Press.

Burgess, Ruth, and Polhill, Chris, 2004, *Eggs and Ashes: Practical and Liturgical Resources for Lent and Holy Week*, Glasgow, Wild Goose Publications.

Celebrating Common Prayer: A Version of the Daily Office SSF, 1995, London, Mowbray.

Farwell, James, 2005, *This is the Night: Suffering Salvation, and the Liturgies of Holy Week*, London, T and T Clark International.

Harnan, Nicholas, 1992, *The Heart's Journey Home: A Quest for Wisdom*, Notre Dame, IN, Ave Maria Press.

Harter, Michael, SJ (ed.), 2005, *Hearts on Fire: Praying with Jesuits*, Chicago, Loyola Press.

John of the Cross, 'Stanzas of the soul' in *The Collected Works of St John of the Cross*, trans. Kieran Kavanaugh, OCD, and Otilio Rodriguez, OCD, Washington, DC, Washington Province of Discalced Carmelites, ICS Publications.

Lewis, Alan E., 2001, *Between Cross and Resurrection: A Theology of Holy Saturday*, Cambridge, MA, Eerdmans.

Maharay, Nisargadatta, 1992, *I Am That*, Acorn Press. Quoted in Daniel J. O'Leary, 2004, *Travelling Light: Your Journey to Wholeness*, Blackrock, Co. Dublin, Columba Press.

Maloney, George A., SJ, 1979, *Invaded by God: Mysticism and the Indwelling Trinity*, Denville, NJ, Dimension Books.

Maloney, George A., SJ, 1993, *Be Filled with the Fullness of God: Living in the Indwelling Trinity*, New York, New City Press.

Merton, Thomas, 1989, *A Merton Reader*, ed. Thomas P. McDonnell, New York, Image Books.

Nouwen, Henri J. M., 2001, *Return of the Prodigal Son*, London, Darton, Longman & Todd.

Oliver, Mary, 1986, 'The journey' in *Dream Work*, Atlantic Monthly Press. Quoted in Daniel J. O'Leary, 2004, *Travelling Light: Your Journey to Wholeness*, Blackrock, Co. Dublin, Columba Press.

Paynter, Neil (ed.), 2001, *Lent and Easter Readings from Iona*, The Iona Community, Wild Goose Publications.

Ramon, Brother, SSF, 1999, *The Flame of Sacred Love: The Divine Fire in Human Experience*, Oxford, Bible Reading Fellowship.

Rinpoche, Sogyal, 1992, *The Tibetan Book of Living and Dying*, San Francisco, CA, Harper.

Rohr, Richard, and Martos, Joseph, 1991, *The Wild Man's Journey: Reflections on Male Spirituality*, Cincinnati, OH, St Anthony Messenger Press.

Searcy, Edwin (ed.), 2003, *Prayers of Walter Brueggemann: Awed to Heaven, Rooted in Earth*, Minneapolis, MN, Fortress.

Solzhenitsyn, Alexander, *The Gulag Archipelago*. Quoted in Daniel J. O'Leary, 2004, *Travelling Light: Your Journey to Wholeness*, Blackrock, Co. Dublin, Columba Press.

Wallis, Ian, 2000, *Holy Saturday Faith: Rediscovering the Legacy of Jesus*, London, SPCK.

Williams, Rowan, et al., 2001, *Darkness Yielding: Angles on Christmas, Holy Week and Easter*, Harlech, Cairns Publications.